T0318951

# Cambridge Elements ≡

**Elements in American Politics**
edited by
Frances E. Lee
*Princeton University*

# AMERICAN AFFECTIVE POLARIZATION IN COMPARATIVE PERSPECTIVE

Noam Gidron
*Hebrew University of Jerusalem*

James Adams
*University of California, Davis*

Will Horne
*Princeton University*

CAMBRIDGE
UNIVERSITY PRESS

# CAMBRIDGE
### UNIVERSITY PRESS

University Printing House, Cambridge CB2 8BS, United Kingdom

One Liberty Plaza, 20th Floor, New York, NY 10006, USA

477 Williamstown Road, Port Melbourne, VIC 3207, Australia

314–321, 3rd Floor, Plot 3, Splendor Forum, Jasola District Centre, New Delhi – 110025, India

79 Anson Road, #06–04/06, Singapore 079906

Cambridge University Press is part of the University of Cambridge.

It furthers the University's mission by disseminating knowledge in the pursuit of education, learning, and research at the highest international levels of excellence.

www.cambridge.org
Information on this title: www.cambridge.org/9781108823449
DOI: 10.1017/9781108914123

© Noam Gidron, James Adams and Will Horne 2020

First published 2020

*A catalogue record for this publication is available from the British Library.*

ISBN 978-1-108-82344-9 Paperback
ISSN 2515-1606 (online)
ISSN 2515-1592 (print)

Additional resources for this publication at www.cambridge.org/gidron

# American Affective Polarization in Comparative Perspective

Elements in American Politics

DOI: 10.1017/9781108914123
First published online: November 2020

Noam Gidron
*Hebrew University of Jerusalem*

James Adams
*University of California, Davis*

Will Horne
*Princeton University*

**Author for correspondence:** Noam Gidron, noam.gidron@mail.huji.ac.il

**Abstract:** American political observers express increasing concern about affective polarization (i.e., partisans' resentment toward political opponents). We advance debates about America's partisan divisions by comparing affective polarization in the USA over the past twenty-five years with affective polarization in nineteen other Western publics. We conclude that American affective polarization is not extreme in comparative perspective, although Americans' dislike of partisan opponents has increased more rapidly since the mid 1990s than in most other Western publics. We then show that affective polarization is more intense when unemployment and inequality are high; when political elites clash over cultural issues such as immigration and national identity; and in countries with majoritarian electoral institutions. Our findings situate American partisan resentment and hostility in comparative perspective and illuminate correlates of affective polarization that are difficult to detect when examining the American case in isolation.

**Keywords:** polarization, inequality, ideology, institutions, public opinion

ISBNs: 9781108823449 (PB), 9781108914123 (OC)
ISSNs: 2515-1606 (online), ISSN 2515-1592 (print)

# Contents

# 1 Introduction

American academics and political commentators express increasing concern about political polarization, especially polarization rooted in distrust, dislike, and contempt between ordinary people across party lines. Americans display growing hostility toward political opponents: in a recent poll, 40 percent of those who self-identify as Democrats or Republicans agreed with the proposition that those in the opposing party "are not just worse for politics – they are downright evil" (Kalmoe and Mason 2019). Americans also display growing unwillingness to form close relationships with people from across the partisan divide: "In 1960, only about 5 percent of partisans reported displeasure at the prospect of interparty marriage; by 2010, that number had increased tenfold, to about 50 percent" (Lelkes 2016, 402). Americans' current levels of distrust and hostility toward partisan opponents have prompted one prominent scholar to argue that "partyism [prejudice toward partisan opponents] is now worse than racism" (Sunstein 2015, 2). This hostility toward partisan opponents, coupled with attachments to their own preferred party, is commonly labeled *affective polarization* (e.g., Hetherington et al. 2016; Iyengar et al. 2012; Mason 2015).

Because scholarly studies of affective polarization overwhelmingly highlight the United States, one might infer that Americans display exceptionally intense hostility and distrust toward political opponents. Yet concerns about partisan animosity extend across Western democracies. Britain has been roiled for the past several years by bitter political divisions over the process of Brexit, the country's historic departure from the European Union (Bale et al. 2019; Hobolt et al. 2020). Many European countries have seen the rise of radical right parties which express contempt for establishment politics, and which in turn prompt intense dislike from establishment opponents (Gidron et al. 2019a, 2019b; Helbling and Jungkunz 2020; Mudde and Kaltwasser 2018). France, for instance, features widespread support for the National Front, a radical right party that strongly opposes multiculturalism and immigration, and which many believe promotes racism and intolerance. Italian politics has been destabilized by the (Northern) League Party and its charismatic Federal Secretary, Matteo Salvini, a hard-line Eurosceptic politician who expresses contempt for established political parties while promoting a nativist message emphasizing opposition to globalization, to illegal immigration, and to the European Union's handling of the foreign refugee crisis. German politics has likewise been destabilized by the rise of the Alternative for Germany (AfD), a populist, radical right party that conjures up uneasy memories of Germany's National Socialist (Nazi) past. Spain, the United

Kingdom, and Canada feature political parties promoting regional independence movements that seek to – literally – split their countries apart. While much has been written about America's affective polarization, we know relatively little about how the US case compares with affective polarization in those countries.

The urgent need to assess America's current democratic challenges has recently prompted engagement between American and comparative politics scholars interested in radicalism, populism, and democratic erosion (e.g., Bonikowski 2017; Hawkins and Littvay 2019; Levitsky and Ziblatt 2018).[1] We extend this Americanist-comparativist conversation to analyze affective polarization, with its pernicious implications for Western democracies' social fabrics. Broadening the scope of polarization research can identify the conditions that intensify partisan animosity, and may highlight factors that can help temper it. As Iyengar et al. (2019, 143) note in a recent review of affective polarization research, "more work is needed to build bridges between Americanists and comparativists interested in these topics."

Our Element provides a bird's-eye view of affective polarization in the United States compared to other Western democracies, and considers political, economic, and institutional factors that help explain differences in affective polarization levels and trends across Western publics. By cross-nationally analyzing Western democracies, we address several pressing questions about American politics, including: Is the US public more affectively polarized than other Western publics? Is America's intensifying affective polarization unusual, or is it part of a general increase across Western democracies? And: What do the cross-national and temporal patterns we identify imply about the predictors of affective polarization, in the United States and abroad?

To answer these questions, we analyze country-level variations in affective polarization and explore how economic, political, and institutional factors shape the emotional climate of politics. More specifically, we analyze whether affective polarization across different Western publics – and also within these publics over time since the 1990s – is related to three structural factors: policy disagreements that divide political elites, economic conditions, and political institutions. While scholars have highlighted each of these factors (along with several others), we cannot easily parse out how they relate to affective polarization in analyses limited to the United States; this single case is over-determined. Our analyses across twenty Western

---

[1]  See also Norris and Inglehart 2019; Kuo 2019; Lieberman et al. 2019; McCoy and Somer 2019; Westwood et al. 2018; Weyland and Madrid 2019.

publics enhance our leverage in sorting out how each factor relates to affective polarization *levels* across different Western publics, and, over time, how changes in these factors are related to affective polarization *changes* within these publics. We describe, theorize and investigate how American affective polarization compares to what we find abroad – a stepping-stone for scholars who seek to unravel this causal story.

## 1.1 Theoretical Debates in the Study of Affective Polarization

Recent years have witnessed a burgeoning body of scholarship on American mass-level polarization (Hetherington 2009; Lelkes 2016). At first, this research emphasized ideological polarization, which pertains to citizens' tendencies to hold extreme positions on the conservative–liberal dimension and on specific issues such as economic policy or immigration, and explores whether citizens hold coherent attitudes across different issues (e.g., Baldassarri and Gelman 2008; Fiorina et al. 2005; Hetherington 2009). Another form of polarization is partisan sorting, or the degree to which citizens' partisan identities align with ideology, as when liberals gravitate toward the Democratic Party and conservatives toward the Republican Party (Levendusky 2009), or with social identities such as religion (Mason 2018).

More recently, scholars have emphasized *affective* polarization, focusing on citizens' *feelings* and emotional responses toward political parties (see Iyengar et al. 2019 for a comprehensive review). A mass public's degree of affective polarization is defined by *how strongly the party identifiers in the public prefer their own party to its opponent(s)*, based on their expressed feelings toward the parties. In the American case, this is a measure of how strongly Democratic partisans prefer their party and how strongly they dislike the Republican Party, and vice versa. (As discussed in Section 2, matters are more complicated in other Western democracies, which typically feature several major parties.) Affective polarization thus has two components: how strongly partisans *dislike* other parties, and how strongly they *like* their own party.[2]

Understanding affective polarization is important because it erodes democratic norms and institutions, and diminishes trust in government – especially among partisans of parties that are currently out of power (Hetherington and Rudolph 2015). Levitsky and Ziblatt (2018, 220) observe that "the fundamental problem facing American democracy remains extreme partisan division – one fueled not just by policy differences but by deeper

---

[2] Note that this definition of affective polarization prioritizes *party identifiers'* feelings toward political parties, without considering independents. We will discuss this issue in Section 2.

sources of resentment." Along similar lines, McCoy and Somer (2019, 258) observe that affective polarization "contributes to a growing perception among citizens that the opposing party and their policies pose a threat to the nation or an individual's way of life. Most dangerously for democracy, these perceptions of threat open the door to undemocratic behavior by an incumbent and his/her supporters to stay in power." In this regard, many Americans fear the possible consequences of affective polarization: a recent Rasmussen survey found that 31 percent of Americans agreed with the proposition that the United States will descend into civil war within five years[3] – apprehensions that are likely fueled by the spectacle of cross-party distrust and hostility.

Beyond its threat to democratic norms and institutions, there are reasons to worry about the social, economic, and political implications of affective polarization. Intense partisan animosity prompts preferential treatment of co-partisans (Lelkes and Westwood 2017), and polarized partisans are more likely to discriminate against partisan opponents in economic transactions (Carlin and Love 2018; McConnell et al. 2018). There is also contemporary evidence that affective polarization and partisan divisions have shaped Americans' perceptions of how the Trump administration responded to the coronavirus outbreak (Druckman et al. 2020), that it has prompted a partisan divide over the health benefits of face masks and social distancing, and even about the severity of this health crisis.[4] However, while there is a consensus that American affective polarization has intensified over the past decades, we know less about the factors that drive this process.

Scholars' explanations for America's intensifying affective polarization reflect the lenses through which they analyze this phenomenon. Political psychology research, and specifically social identity theory, emphasizes peoples' tendencies to form groups and then protect their group's status, with partisanship being a crucial group identity in contemporary politics (Huddy et al. 2015). This approach suggests that partisans are like sports fans, cheering for their team and against its opponents (Mason 2018; Miller and Conover 2015). From this perspective, growing attachment to partisan identities, rather than ideological worldviews or specific issue positions, drives American affective polarization.

---

[3] Rasmussen Report. "31% Think U.S. Civil War Likely Soon." www.rasmussenreports.com /public_content/politics/general_politics/june_2018/31_think_u_s_civil_war_likely_soon

[4] "Republicans, Democrats Move Even Further Apart in Coronavirus Concerns." www .pewresearch.org/politics/2020/06/25/republicans-democrats-move-even-further-apart-in-coronavirus-concerns/

Social identity theory rests on universal assumptions regarding people's underlying motivations: it takes as its starting point the notion that "*Homo sapiens* is a social species; group affiliation is essential to our sense of self" (Iyengar et al. 2019, 130). Yet notwithstanding its broad assumptions on human behavior, this approach has illuminated academic and public debates focused on specifically *American* politics (Klein 2020; for a comparative application, see Huddy et al. 2018). As noted, we know less about how American affective polarization compares to what we find in other countries.

We adopt a complementary perspective that shifts the focus from universal psychological features to contextual determinants of affective polarization. Building on American and comparative politics research, we emphasize three structural factors that may drive differences over time and space in affective polarization: the intensity and nature of policy-based disagreements that characterize a country's party system; national economic conditions, specifically income inequality and unemployment; and electoral institutions, notably the voting systems countries use to select representatives to their national legislatures.[5]

With respect to policy disputes, there is an ongoing debate about how the widening ideological divide between American political elites relates to intensifying affective polarization in the mass public. Some scholars argue that mass-level affective polarization is linked specifically with elite disputes over cultural issues such as multiculturalism and national identity, which fuel stronger emotions than do economic debates (Hetherington et al. 2016; Sides et al. 2018); others, however, link American affective polarization to economic disagreements (Abramowitz and Webster 2017; Iyengar et al. 2012). Yet this question is not easily settled by analyzing American politics in isolation, which is why we extend our analyses across Western democracies. As we write this in August 2020, at the outset of America's general presidential election campaign, this issue of cultural disagreements appears highly pertinent in light of the ongoing nation-wide protests in support of racial justice and the Black Lives Matter movement, which has sparked a wider cultural debate over questions relating to race, police funding and broader questions over interpretations of America's history. In a July 4th speech delivered at Mt. Rushmore, President Trump starkly framed these types of "cultural war" debates as a defining political and social divide in America, asserting that "Our nation is witnessing a merciless campaign to wipe out our history, defame our heroes, erase our values and indoctrinate our children . . .

---

[5] There are additional structural factors that may influence affective polarization, such as media markets (Lelkes et al. 2017). We discuss these issues, and how they open more avenues for comparative polarization research, in the Conclusions section.

Angry mobs are trying to tear down statues of our founders, deface our most sacred memorials and unleash a wave of violent crime in our cities."[6] To the extent that such cultural issues feature prominently in the 2020 presidential election campaign, it is important to understand whether such cultural debates fuel mass-level partisan hostility and distrust. If the answer is "yes" – which is the empirical pattern we document in this Element – we might expect the 2020 presidential election campaign to further intensify American affective polarization, all else being equal.

With respect to the effects of economic conditions, scholars argue that America's growing income inequality drives affective polarization in the mass public (Stewart et al. 2020), while comparative politics research suggests that economic downturns – such as the global economic recession that began in 2008 – incite more adversarial political interactions, independently of the effects of income inequality (Kriesi and Hutter 2019). While economic conditions have not been extensively studied in the affective polarization literature so far, we present evidence that they are closely linked with partisan affective evaluations. This finding, too, is relevant to contemporary Western politics given that the COVID-19 pandemic has plunged much of the world – including the United States – into a recession, which some economists project could last for several years.

With respect to political institutions, scholars argue that America's majoritarian political system – which is sustained in part by a single-winner, plurality-based voting system to elect public officials – encourages partisans to view politics as a zero-sum struggle, prompting them to despise opponents who (they fear) will take all if their own party is defeated (Drutman 2019). In the American context, this belief led to the coining of the term "the Flight 93 election," which compared the potential presidential election of Hillary Clinton in 2016 to the high-jacking of an airplane, in which Republicans needed to "Charge the cockpit or die" (Anton 2016). By contrast, institutions that support many parties and encourage political compromise – notably proportional representation voting systems – may promote what Arend Lijphart (2010) labels "kinder, gentler" politics, that defuse tensions between opponents. Since electoral institutions are practically constant over time in most countries (including in the United States), we evaluate these arguments by comparing affective polarization levels between countries that feature different voting systems.

In the following sections, we document affective polarization levels and trends in the United States and nineteen other Western democracies. We will

---

[6] "Trump Uses Mount Rushmore Speech to Deliver Divisive Culture War Message." *New York Times*, July 5, 2020. www.nytimes.com/2020/07/03/us/politics/trump-coronavirus-mount-rushmore.html?action=click&module=Top%20Stories&pgtype=Homepage

then examine how the three structural factors discussed – elite-level policy disputes, national economic conditions, and electoral laws – can help explain which countries display more versus less intense affective polarization levels, and also how affective polarization fluctuates within countries over time. Before we move to the empirical analyses, we briefly preview our key findings.

## 1.2 Plan of the Element, and our Key Findings

### 1.2.1 Situating America's Afective Polarization in Comparative Perspective

Our Element's first part, which analyzes affective polarization levels and trends across twenty Western publics over the past twenty-five years, situates the American public in comparative perspective, in an effort to answer two questions: How affectively polarized is the United States compared to other Western democracies? And: Is America's intensifying affective polarization unusual, or is it part of a general increase across Western publics? To address these questions, we analyze over eighty national election surveys across twenty Western publics between 1996 and 2017, which include common questions eliciting respondents' party identifications along with the warmth of their feelings toward each major party in their country, which respondents rate on a "feeling thermometer scale." We use these survey responses to compute an overall *affective polarization score* for the respondents in each election survey, which is our measure of the intensity of affective polarization in that country in that election year. By analyzing these scores across countries, we can compare the *levels* (intensity) of affective polarization across different Western publics; by comparing these scores across different survey years in the same country, we can track over-time *trends* in affective polarization for each public in our study. We are particularly interested in comparing affective polarization levels and trends in the United States with those in the other nineteen countries in our study, which bear on the questions posed. These analyses support the following conclusions.

*Affective polarization in the United States is not unduly intense compared with other Western publics.* While America's current affective polarization level is somewhat more intense than the average (and the median) level across our twenty Western publics, it is neither at nor near the top. In fact, the US public appears significantly *less* affectively polarized than the Greek, Portuguese, and Spanish publics; *about as* polarized as the publics in Australia, Britain, France, and New Zealand; but substantially *more* affectively polarized than the Dutch public along with most of the Scandinavian publics. Although most affective polarization research analyzes the United States, the American public is not an outlier among Western democracies (see also Lauka et al. 2018; Wagner 2020; Reiljan 2020).

*Since the mid 1990s, affective polarization has intensified more sharply in the United States than in most other Western publics.* Consistent with previous research (e.g., Boxell et al. 2020; Iyengar et al. 2019), we find that American affective polarization has intensified over time, and moreover, that this rise is driven by Americans' growing dislike of partisan opponents, rather than by warming attachments to their own party. Furthermore, our comparative analyses suggest that America's intensifying affective polarization is *not* part of a cross-national trend: instead we find that affective polarization in other Western publics has remained steady (on average) across this period, intensifying in some publics (notably Greece and Portugal), diminishing in others (including Canada), and remaining stable in most.

*Compared with other Western publics, American partisans tend to dislike other parties more intensely and like their own parties less.* Because affective polarization represents the difference between partisans' feelings for their own party versus its opponent(s), American partisans' comparatively intense dislike of opponents *intensifies* affective polarization, while their comparative lack of enthusiasm for their own party *defuses* affective polarization. We find that the US public is unusual both in partisans' intense hostility toward opponents and in their lukewarm feelings for their own party, but that the American public is *not* unusual in terms of the difference between their in-party liking and their out-party dislike – that is, America's overall level of affective polarization is not an outlier among Western publics. Section 2 reports the analyses that support these conclusions, and delineates some important caveats relating to questions about whether our survey-based measures of affective polarization levels are cross-nationally and temporally comparable.

Taken together, our analyses suggest that when considering affective polarization in comparative perspective, America's glass is less than half full. The good news is that, compared to other Western publics, the United States is not excessively polarized, being only slightly more affectively polarized than the median public in our twenty-country study. The bad news is, first, that over the past twenty-plus years affective polarization has intensified more sharply in the United States than in most other Western publics; second, that this trend reflects American partisans' increasing hostility toward opponents, rather than growing warmth toward their own party. Intuitively, affective polarization fueled by partisans' intense dislike (even hatred) of opponents seems to pose greater political and social risks than do stronger attachments to one's own side.

### 1.2.2 Explaining Variations in Affective Polarization

Section 2 documents relationships between affective polarization and three structural factors which scholars have theorized may correlate with affective polarization: *elite-level policy disagreements, national economic conditions, and electoral institutions*. We document the following relationships.

*Affective polarization changes in mass publics are related to elite-level conflicts on cultural issues.* In analyzing affective polarization trends within countries over time, we find that as party elites become more polarized over cultural issues such as immigration, race, and national identity, affective polarization tends to intensify, in analyses that hold economic conditions and electoral institutions constant. In particular, the Unites States, which displays the sharpest increase in elite cultural polarization across the period of our study, has also affectively polarized at the mass level. By contrast, we find no evidence that changes in elite economic polarization track changes in affective polarization.

*Adverse economic conditions are linked with more intense affective polarization.* We find, first, that affective polarization is more intense in countries with greater income inequality, in analyses that hold elite policy disputes and electoral institutions constant. The Western democracies with the highest income inequality levels include the United States (the most economically unequal country in our study), Portugal, Greece, Britain, and Australia, all of which display relatively intense affective polarization levels. By contrast, the most economically equal countries in our study include the Netherlands and Finland, which display comparatively mild affective polarization. This cross-national pattern resonates with US-based research showing that affective polarization correlates with economic inequality across the American states (Stewart et al. 2020).

Second, we find consistent evidence, in comparisons both between countries and within countries over time, that affective polarization intensifies with higher unemployment. The most affectively polarized countries in our study are Greece, Portugal, and Spain, which all featured comparatively high unemployment across the period of our study, while the Netherlands and Norway are among several countries in our study that featured comparatively low levels of unemployment and affective polarization. Moreover, affective polarization increased sharply across many Western democracies around the time of the global financial crisis, when unemployment spiked. These analyses again are robust to controls for electoral laws and the intensity of elite policy disputes.

*Partisans residing in countries with majoritarian, single-winner voting systems tend to dislike opposition parties more intensely, and like their own party less, than do partisans in countries with proportional voting systems.* We have already noted this pattern of partisans' diminished ratings for *all* parties (both their own party and its opponents) with respect to the United States, which employs the plurality voting system. We find that this pattern extends to all of the countries in our study that select their representatives via single-winner voting systems, namely Canada, the UK, France, and Australia, in addition to the United States. Moreover, we find a consistent cross-national relationship between electoral system proportionality and partisans' warmer feelings toward political parties (their own party and its opponents). These cross-national patterns are in line with Lijphart's (2010) arguments about the "kinder, gentler" politics that characterize the compromise-oriented, multiparty systems with proportional representation. As we noted previously, this general pattern need not affect the overall intensity of affective polarization, which depends on the *difference* between partisans' ratings of their own party versus its opponents – and in fact we detect no significant cross-national relationship between our overall, difference-based affective polarization measure and the proportionality of the voting system. However, to the extent that single-winner voting systems are associated with citizens' diminished liking and trust for political parties in general, this may be cause for concern.

## 1.3 A Note on Inference

Before turning to our substantive sections, we briefly address the types of inferences to be drawn from our research. For reasons discussed in the second half of this Element, we are cautious about inferring cause-and-effect relationships from the empirical patterns we document; that is, we do not claim to conclusively prove that variations in economic conditions, elite cultural polarization, and electoral laws *cause* affective polarization levels in Western publics to rise or fall. We refrain from inferring causation primarily because we cannot adequately account for several factors – beyond the structural influences we analyze – that may influence affective polarization. These potentially confounding factors include countries' democratic histories; political scandals; national media regimes; social, geographic, and linguistic cleavages; and differences across publics' levels of education and political interest. We do, however, believe that the relationships we identify represent an essential first step toward developing causal explanations, and that our findings mark out national economic conditions, elite cultural disputes, and electoral laws as "prime suspects" when investigating the causes of affective polarization.

## 2 Affective Polarization in Comparative Perspective: How Does the American Public Compare?

Political commentators and academics extensively discuss American affective polarization, defined as hostility and resentment across party lines. This America-centric focus implies that the United States displays unusually intense affective polarization. Yet, as discussed in Section 1, we have observed heated political divisions across many Western democracies in recent years, including the rise of divisive, anti-system parties in Germany, France, Italy, and Greece; controversies over Brexit, Britain's historic exit from the European Union; political turmoil in Spain over the issue of the Catalan region's autonomy; contentious regional and linguistic divisions in Belgium and Canada; and bitter political divisions in Australia over the issue of climate policy.

As we write these words in the summer of 2020, the world confronts the COVID-19 virus pandemic, a health crisis that is testing Western publics' faith in their political institutions and leaders, and where citizens' willingness to comply with public safety directives designed to protect both themselves and their fellow citizens, are life-or-death issues. While affective polarization is only one strand of the social fabric, it seems intuitive that partisan distrust and hostility may diminish citizens' concern and empathy for others. In this regard, polling data shows massive partisan gaps in Americans' perceptions of the severity of the crisis, and in individuals' willingness to follow public health directives such as social distancing and wearing face masks.[7]

This section situates America's affective polarization in a comparative study across twenty Western publics, over the time period beginning in 1996 (the first year for which we have extensive, cross-nationally comparable survey data) and ending in 2017 (the most recent year these data are available). Our aim is descriptive: namely we compare the levels and changes in America's affective polarization across this 1996–2017 time period with the levels and changes in nineteen other Western publics. (Section 3 seeks to explain these variations in affective polarization, in the United States and abroad.) We address the questions: How affectively polarized is the US public, compared with other Western publics? And: Is affective polarization intensifying over time across Western democracies, as it has intensified in the United States? We also break down affective polarization into its two components, namely partisans' *dislike* of other parties and their *liking* of their own party, and compare the United States to other Western publics along both dimensions.

---

[7] For example, see https://news.gallup.com/poll/309611/americans-social-distancing-less-vigilant.aspx, conducted April 20–26, 2020.

To address these questions, we first introduce the data set we analyze in this Element, which comprises eighty-one national election surveys across twenty Western democracies that were administered between 1996 and 2017. We present the common questions in each survey that elicit respondents' party identifications and their feelings toward each major political party in their country. We explain how we use these survey responses to construct a measure of the level (i.e., the intensity) of affective polarization for each country in each survey year – defined as how much more warmly partisan survey respondents feel toward their own party compared to its opponents – and how these measured levels can be compared across different Western publics, and also within countries over time. We then situate the United States in comparative perspective, showing that American partisans appear only slightly more affectively polarized than the partisans of the average Western party system, but that Americans' hostility toward partisan opponents has intensified more sharply than in most other Western publics across the 1996–2017 period of our study. Commentators who assert that American politics are becoming increasingly contentious appear to be correct, and in more recent elections (particularly beginning in 2012) the United States has indeed become one of the more affectively polarized Western democracies in our study.

## 2.1 Defining and Measuring Affective Polarization Using Election Survey Data

Political scientists typically define the level of affective polarization in a mass public as the difference between how much partisans (party identifiers) like their own party versus how much they dislike other parties (Iyengar et al. 2012; Mason 2015; Reiljan 2020). Here, we rely on a common question across our election surveys that taps into respondents' affective ratings (i.e., their liking) of different political parties. Thus, in the American case, we analyze survey respondents' ratings of the Democratic and Republican parties; for Britain we analyze respondents' ratings of the Labour, Conservative, and Liberal Democratic parties (among others); and so on. The party thermometer ratings we analyze presumably capture survey respondents' feelings toward party *elites*, rather than toward these parties' rank-and-file *supporters*. While it is unclear which dimension of partisan hostility should concern us the most (i.e., should we be more worried if Democratic and Republican partisans despise their opponent's political leaders, of if they despise their opponent's supporters?), in practice, citizens' feelings toward parties and toward their supporters tend to be correlated, albeit imperfectly. (Druckman and Levendusky 2019). For practical purposes, we have extensive, cross-nationally comparable survey-based measures of citizens' feelings about parties, while lacking comparable measures of their feelings toward these parties' supporters. We therefore analyze survey respondents' expressed feelings toward parties, which likely capture their ratings of party elites, with the expectation that these feelings are related to their attitudes toward these parties' rank and file supporters.

Following the standard definition in the Americanist literature, we define affective polarization as the *difference* between partisans' feelings toward their own party versus its opponents, rather than strictly in terms of feelings toward opponents. According to this conception, a public where partisans despise their opponents while feeling neutral toward their own party is no more affectively polarized than a public whose partisans feel neutral toward rival parties but unconditionally love their own party: in both cases the difference in partisans' feelings toward their party versus its opponents is the same.

There are theoretical and practical reasons for adopting a difference-based affective polarization measure. Theoretically, partisans' willingness to engage in hostile, politically motivated behavior may depend on how much they prefer their own party to its opponents. This applies to economic discrimination (i.e., "I prefer to hire a fellow Democrat for this job, not a Republican," or "I prefer to rent my house to a Republican, not a Democrat"), and also to partisans' tolerance for discriminatory behavior by their party's elites (i.e., "I am glad my party's elected officials passed voting laws that suppress turnout among the types of people who support my opponents"). Practically, the difference-based affective polarization measure helps mitigate the problem of variations in how survey respondents interpret the party like/dislike questions we analyze. As will be discussed, these questions ask respondents to rate the warmth of their feelings toward different parties on a 0 to 10 'thermometer scale,' where higher numbers denote warmer feelings. However this raises a problem when comparing party ratings across respondents, because different respondents may interpret these numbers in different ways: for instance one respondent who feels warmly toward a party may assign it a thermometer score of 9 (near the maximum score of 10), while another respondent who feels equally warmly may assign the party a score of 7, because she interprets the scale differently. This problem, which scholars label "differential item functioning", may be especially severe when comparing affective polarization levels cross-nationally (as we will do later in this section), since there may be different cultural norms in how citizens from different countries respond to these like/dislike questions. Defining affective polarization as the *difference* between survey respondents' expressed warmth toward their own party versus its opponents mitigates some of these problems. As Lelkes and Westwood (2017, 489) explain when justifying a difference-based affective polarization measure: "relying on difference scores, rather than raw feeling thermometer scores, helps ameliorate the differential item functioning of feeling thermometers."[8]

### 2.1.1 Survey Questions and Variable Construction

We measure affective polarization using survey data about citizens' partisanship and their feelings toward political parties, obtained from the Comparative Study of Electoral Systems (CSES). The CSES has fielded a common module of questions across the national election studies administered in fifty-six countries beginning in 1996 and available (to date) through 2017. Our study encompasses eighty-one surveys administered around the times of national elections in the twenty Western democracies included in the CSES. Besides the United States, our study includes surveys from Australia, Austria, Canada, Denmark, Finland, France, Germany, Great Britain, Greece, Iceland, Ireland, Israel, the Netherlands, New Zealand, Norway, Portugal, Spain, Sweden, and Switzerland. We do not analyze post-communist Eastern European countries, which feature very different political traditions (Pop-Eleches and Tucker 2011).[9]

The CSES is appropriate for our study because every CSES survey includes a common module of questions that elicit the information required to measure affective polarization, namely respondents' party identifications (if any), and their feelings toward the major parties in their political system. The party identification question reads: "Do you usually think of yourself as close to any particular party? If so, which one?" Respondents who replied "no" were then asked: "Do you feel yourself a little closer to one of the political parties than the others?" We code as party supporters both those who feel close and those who feel a little closer to the relevant party.[10]

For our measure of partisans' feelings toward the parties in their country, we relied on a CSES survey question asking respondents to rate each party on a 0–10 "thermometer" scale. The question is: "I'd like to know what you think about each of our political parties. After I read the name of a political party, please rate it

---

[8] Alternative measures of partisan animosity include thermometer ratings of out-partisans (rather than out-parties), preferences for social distance (such as willingness to marry someone from the outgroup), and stereotypes toward opposing partisans (Druckman and Levendusky 2019). Moreover, experimental work analyzes discrimination towards out-partisans using economic decision-making games (Carlin and Love 2018; Sheffer 2020; Westwood et al. 2018). Unfortunately, we lack extensive temporal, cross-nationally comparable data based on these measures, and therefore rely on party thermometer scores.

[9] For comparative affective polarization analyses including Central and Eastern Europe, see Reiljan (2020) and Harteveld (2019), who document relatively intense polarization in this region.

[10] We cannot distinguish between strong and weak partisans due to challenges of over-time and cross-national data comparability across the CSES surveys (Klar et al. 2018).

on a scale from 0 to 10, where 0 means you strongly dislike that party and 10 means that you strongly like that party." To Make interpretations intuitive, we present results in which the feeling thermometer is reversed such that a rating of 10 denotes to most intense negative party evaluation and 0 the most positive. This simplifies the interpretation of our results: higher levels of the affective polarization variable we construct denote more intense affective polarization.

### 2.1.2 Computing the Level of Affective Polarization for a Country-Year Election Survey

*Affective polarization in the two-party US system.* As discussed, our measure of affective polarization in a public in a given year is the difference between partisans' expressed feelings toward their own party, on average, versus their feelings toward rival parties, on average, based on the set of Comparative Study of Electoral Systems (CSES) survey responses for that country-year. For the United States, which features two dominant parties, this is the average difference between the thermometer scores that all self-identified Democratic and Republican partisans in the survey assigned to their own party versus the score they assigned to its opponent.[11]

To illustrate how our affective polarization measure works in the United States, consider the 2016 American CSES survey, administered shortly after the bitter presidential election campaign between Hillary Clinton and Donald Trump. In this election, the Democratic candidate, Clinton, won slightly over 51 percent of the two-party vote, while the Republican candidate, Trump, won slightly less than 49 percent. Based on the CSES survey responses we analyze, both partisan constituencies, as expected, strongly preferred their own party, which we label their *in-party*, to their opponent which we label the *out-party*: Republican partisans assigned their Republican in-party a warm average score of 2.69 on the 0–10 thermometer scale (where 0 denotes the warmest feelings), but assigned the Democratic out-party a chilly average thermometer score of 7.30; thus the difference between Republican partisans' out-party and in-party ratings is $(7.30 - 2.69)$ = 4.61 units on the thermometer scale. Democratic partisans assigned their in-party a mean score of 2.45 but assigned the Republican out-party a mean score of 7.21, a difference of $(7.21 - 2.45)$ = 4.76 units. The measured level (intensity) of affective polarization for the US public in 2016, computed from these CSES data, is the average of the thermometer score differentials for Republican partisans and

---

[11] These computations are over all respondents who provided valid thermometer ratings of both parties (i.e., we omit responsnts who did not answer or who answered "don't know"). We exclude partisans of minor US parties (the Greens, the Libertarian Party, etc.), which CSES respondents were not asked to rate on the thermometer scale.

Democratic partisans, weighted by the vote share that each party received. We demonstrate how we construct this variable in Table 1.

The larger the average difference between CSES partisans' thermometer ratings of their in-party versus their out-party(ies), the higher the measured level of affective polarization. We show that 4.69, the computed level for the US public in 2016, is well above the average measured affective polarization level among the twenty Western publics in our study.

### 2.1.3 Affective Polarization in Multiparty Systems

While defining and measuring affective polarization levels is straightforward in the American two-party system, it is not obvious how to compare the United States to other Western democracies, which typically feature three or more major parties (i.e., these are *multiparty democracies*). When comparing America's affective polarization level to that of the multiparty German system, for instance, should the relevant comparison be limited to the thermometer ratings that the supporters of the two largest German parties (the leftist Social Democratic Party and the more conservative Christian Democratic Party) assigned to their own party and to its largest opponent, or should the German measure incorporate partisans' ratings of *all* the significant parties in their system – which includes the Greens, The Left Party (Die Linke), the Free Democratic Party, and the Alternative for Germany?

**Table 1** Average party thermometer ratings for Democratic and Republican party identifiers, 2016 American election study

|  | Average in-party rating (1) | Average out-party rating (2) | Two-party vote share | Difference between out-party and in-party ratings (3) |
|---|---|---|---|---|
| Democratic partisans | 2.45 | 7.21 | 0.51 | 7.21 − 2.45 = 4.76 |
| Republican partisans | 2.69 | 7.30 | 0.49 | 7.30 − 2.69 = 4.61 |

Weighted average difference between partisans' in-party ratings and out-party ratings $(4.76 * 0.51) + (4.61 * 0.49) = 4.69$

*Notes.* Table 1 reports the mean ratings that self-identified Democratic and Republican partisans assigned to their own party (the in-party) and to its opponent (the out-party) on a 0-to-10 thermometer scale. For our computations we have reversed the scale endpoints, so that 0 denotes the warmest feelings and 10 denotes the coldest feelings. The computations are for the American respondents from the 2016 American module of the Comparative Study of Electoral Systems (CSES)

To address this issue, we adopt the following measure, developed by Reiljan (2020): we weight the feelings of *all* relevant parties' partisans, and we define each partisan's feelings toward out-parties as the weighted average thermometer rating they assign to *all* out-parties in their system, where these weights are proportional to each out-party's size, based on its national vote share at the current election.[12] We use this formula to compute the difference-based affective polarization level for each partisan constituency in the CSES country-year election survey, and we define the affective polarization score for the public as a whole as the average of each partisan constituency's affective polarization level, weighted by party size. *Intuitively, this affective polarization measure represents how much we expect a randomly selected partisan to prefer their own party to a randomly selected out-party, where the odds of selecting each out-party are proportional to its size.*

Our multiparty affective polarization measure has the desirable properties of weighing all partisans' feelings toward all parties in the system, while also accounting for parties' varying sizes. This is important because the partisans in multiparty systems frequently express much colder (warmer) feelings toward some out-parties than others, and it is advisable to account for such variations. For instance, in Germany, the supporters of the leftist Social Democratic Party often express much warmer feelings toward the leftist, ecologically oriented Green Party than they do toward either the rightist Christian Democratic Party (CDU) or (especially) toward the radical right Alternative for Germany (AfD). However, given that some parties are much larger than others (for instance the German CDU is much larger than the Greens and Die Linke), our measure adjusts for different parties' sizes so that partisans' expressed hostility toward a small, politically divisive party on the fringes of the political system do not weigh as heavily in computing the affective polarization scores as do partisans' feelings toward large, mainstream out-parties. Thus our multiparty affective polarization scores account for every partisan constituency's expressed feelings toward every relevant out-party, while giving greater weight to the larger, more politically significant parties in the system.

### 2.1.4 Technical Details of the Formulas for Computing Affective Polarization Scores

For interested readers, we present mathematical expressions for our computations of affective polarization scores that formalize the intuitive explanation

---

[12] We weight the ratings of all parties that CSES respondents were asked to rate on the thermometer scales, which typically include all parties whose national vote shares exceed one or two percentage points.

presented. Non-technical readers may safely skip this subsection and move directly to the next section, which reports cross-national comparisons of affective polarization levels across Western publics.

*Computing the affective polarization level for a given partisan constituency.* Consider a party system with parties A, B, ..., K. The difference-based affective polarization score for party A's partisans in a given country-election survey, labelled [Affective Polarization Party A], is given by the formula:

Affective Polarization Party A =

$$\sum_{i=B}^{K}(|\text{Party A's In-Party Thermometer Score} - \text{Party A's Out-Party Thermometer}$$

$$\text{Score}_i|) * (\text{Vote Share Party}_i * (1 - \text{Vote Share Party A})) \qquad (1)$$

Where:

Party A's In-Party Thermometer Score = The mean thermometer rating that party A's partisans assign to their in-party, i.e., to Party A.

Party A's Out-Party Thermometer Score ($i$) = The mean thermometer rating that party A's partisans assign to the out-party $i$.

Vote share Party ($i$) = Party $i$'s national vote share in the current parliamentary election.

This measure represents the average of how much partisans of Party A prefer their in-party to all out-parties, weighted by these out-parties' relative sizes.[13]

The overall affective polarization score for a given country-year CSES survey is the average of each partisan constituency's affective polarization level, weighted by its vote share:

Country Level Affective Polarization

$$= \sum_{i=A}^{K}(\text{Affective Polarization Party}_i * \text{vote Share Party}_i) \qquad (2)$$

### 2.1.5 Case Selection and Descriptive Statistics

Table 2 lists the eighty-one Comparative Study of Electoral Systems (CSES) surveys from twenty Western democracies, across the period 1996–2017, that we analyze in our study. Appendix 2.1 lists the parties in each country that CSES respondents were asked to rate on the thermometer scales. As discussed,

---

[13] We normalize the total vote share captured by the parties that the CSES respondents were asked to rate. For example, if the parties included in the CSES survey captured 97 percent of the vote, we divide each party's vote share by 0.97 to make scores comparable across countries.

**Table 2** CSES country-year election surveys included in our
study

| Country | Elections included |
| --- | --- |
| Australia | 1996, 2004, 2007, 2013 |
| Austria | 2008, 2013, 2017 |
| Canada | 1997, 2004, 2008, 2011, 2015 |
| Denmark | 1998, 2001, 2007 |
| Finland | 2003, 2007, 2011 |
| France | 2002, 2007, 2012 |
| Germany | 1998, 2002, 2005, 2009, 2013, 2017 |
| Great Britain | 1997, 2005, 2015 |
| Greece | 2009, 2012, 2015 |
| Iceland | 1999, 2003, 2007, 2009, 2013 |
| Ireland | 2002, 2007, 2011, 2016 |
| Israel | 1996, 2003, 2006, 2013 |
| Netherlands | 1998, 2002, 2006, 2010 |
| New Zealand | 1996, 2002, 2008, 2011, 2014 |
| Norway | 1997, 2001, 2005, 2009, 2013 |
| Portugal | 2002, 2005, 2009, 2015 |
| Spain | 1996, 2000, 2004, 2008 |
| Sweden | 1998, 2002, 2006, 2014 |
| Switzerland | 1999, 2003, 2007, 2011 |
| **United States** | **1996, 2004, 2008, 2012, 2016** |

*Notes.* Table 2 lists the countries and elections included in our data
set, which comprise all the currently available election surveys
from the Comparative Study of Electoral Systems across the
twenty Western democracies in our study.

these surveys are timed to coincide with national elections to the country's
lower house of parliament, which are typically held every four to five years
(although the period may be shorter if the parliament is dissolved early). We
note, however, that the CSES did not administer survey modules for every
national election in every county in our study across the 1996–2017 period.
However the CSES is the most comprehensive cross-national data set suitable
for comparative affective polarization analyses.

There are five available American CSES surveys, from 1996, 2004, 2008,
2012, and 2016, not including the 2000 election. We note that the 2000
American National Election Study (ANES) does ask respondents to rate
parties on a 0–100 thermometer scale, so we considered incorporating this

survey into our study. However this question appears in a pre-election survey, while all CSES modules are administered in the weeks following each election. We are uncomfortable comparing pre- and post-electoral survey data, as responses given during an electoral campaign may differ from those after the campaign has ended (Sheffer 2020). Hence we do not include the 2000 American election in our study.

For each CSES election survey we compute the difference-based polarization score, described previously, which we take as the measured affective polarization level in the country in the survey year. Table 3 presents descriptive statistics for our difference-based affective polarization variable (row 1), and for the variable's two components, out-party dislike (row 2) and in-party liking (row 3). Recall that we reverse the thermometer scale for the out-party dislike variable, so that higher scores denote more negative feelings toward out-parties; however, for the in-party liking variable, we keep the original ordering of the thermometer so that higher values denote more positive feelings. To recapitulate: higher values on the difference-based affective polarization variable denote more intense affective polarization; higher values on the out-party dislike variable stand for more *negative* out-party evaluations; and higher values on the in-party liking variable denote more *positive* affective evaluations.

As displayed in Table 3, the average computed affective polarization level across the eighty-one CSES surveys in the twenty countries in our study is 4.38; that is, on average, partisans assigned their own party a thermometer rating between 4 and 5 units higher than the (weighted) average rating they assigned to out-parties, on the 0-to-10 thermometer scale. The standard deviation is 0.57 units, suggesting considerable variation in the intensity of

**Table 3** Descriptive statistic of affective polarization levels (N = 81)

| | Mean | Standard deviation | Minimum | Maximum |
|---|---|---|---|---|
| *Affective polarization* | 4.38 | 0.57 | 2.69 | 5.70 |
| *Out-party dislike* | 6.28 | 0.65 | 4.80 | 7.85 |
| *In-party liking* | 8.13 | 0.42 | 7.12 | 8.94 |

*Notes*. Table 3 reports descriptive statistics on the levels of difference-based affective polarization (row 1; higher values denote more intense affective polarization), out-party dislike (row 2; higher values denote greater out-party dislike), and in-party liking (row 3; higher values denote greater in-party liking), computed on the eighty-one Comparative Study of Electoral Systems (CSES) election surveys listed earlier in Table 2. The variable definitions are given in the text.

affective polarization across time and place. The minimum affective polarization level, 2.69, was computed for the Netherlands in 2006 and denotes that the self-identified Dutch partisans in the 2006 CSES survey, on average, assigned their in-party a thermometer rating of less than 3 units above their (weighted) average out-party rating (i.e., the Dutch public in 2006 was *not* affectively polarized, in comparative perspective). The highest computed affective polarization level, 5.70, was for Portugal in 2015, and denotes that, on average, Portuguese partisans assigned in-party thermometer scores that were nearly six points higher than the (weighted) average scores they assigned to out-parties (i.e., Portugal appears intensely affectively polarized in 2015, compared with other Western publics). The highest computed affective polarization level in the United States was 4.97 in 2012, and the lowest US level was 4.01 in 2008.

Turning to the two components of our difference-based affective polarization measure, the mean out-party dislike score across the CSES surveys was 6.28, on the 0-to-10 thermometer scale where 10 denotes maximum dislike and 5 denotes neutral feelings. This 6.28 average score implies that the partisans in our twenty democracies expressed somewhat negative (hostile) feelings toward out-parties, on average. The lowest (i.e., least intense) out-party dislike score, 4.80, was for the Netherlands in 2006, and is near the neutral point (5) of the thermometer scale. The highest dislike score, 7.85, was computed for Greece in 2012. The standard deviation of the computed mean out-party dislike scores across the eighty-one election surveys in our study is 0.65.

With respect to in-party liking, the mean score across our elections surveys is 8.13, where higher values denote more positive affective evaluations. The minimum computed in-party liking score was 7.12 for Norway in 2011. Note that even this "least positive" 7.12 in-party thermometer rating is still quite warm on the 0-to-10 thermometer scale, indicating that partisans in Western publics invariably express warmth toward their own party. The highest mean in-party liking score was for Switzerland in 2007, 8.94, which approaches the warmest value on the scale (10). The standard deviation of the eighty-one mean in-party liking scores in our study is only 0.42, well below the standard deviation of the mean out-party dislike scores (0.65), indicating the mean in-party liking scores are fairly similar across the countries and election surveys in our study, while there is more variation in mean out-party dislike. This pattern plausibly arises because party identifiers almost invariably feel warmly toward their own party (else they would not identify with it!) while they need not invariably dislike out-parties: partisans may feel neutral toward some out-parties or even like them, albeit not as much as they like their own party.

For the United States, the highest computed out-party dislike score is 7.25 in 2016, the most recent US election in our study, and reflects the intensifying hostility that Democratic and Republican partisans express toward each other; this 7.25 value is the seventh-highest out-party dislike level among the eighty-one country-year observations in our study. All but one of the elections with higher levels of out-party dislike than the United States in 2016 took place in Portugal, Greece, and Spain, intensely polarized countries that have faced significant political crises in recent years (we will say more about this in the next section). The other election which displayed more intense levels of out-party dislike was in Canada in 2004, when a major corruption scandal damaged the ruling Liberal Party's reputation. The United States also reached its lowest in-party liking value in 2016, 7.43, the fifth lowest computed level in our study. This denotes that, compared to other Western publics, American partisans in 2016 expressed tepid feelings toward their own party *and* unusually negative (hostile) evaluations of their out-party (i.e., American partisans were comparatively negative toward parties in general, both their own and its opponent).

## 2.2 Cross-National Levels of Affective Polarization: The Un-exceptional United States

We compare cross-national levels of affective polarization, out-party dislike, and in-party liking, using country averages computed across all the Comparative Study of Electoral Systems (CSES) surveys listed in Table 2. Recall that different countries were surveyed in different years, and that some national elections are not covered in the CSES surveys. However we have at least three CSES surveys from each country in our study and, except for Denmark and Spain – for which the most recent CSES surveys are from 2007 and 2008, respectively – every country features at least one CSES survey from both before and from after the onset of the global financial crisis that began in 2008–9.

Figure 1 displays country averages for our difference-based affective polarization measure (Figure 1A) and for its two components, out-party dislike (Figure 1B) and in-party liking (Figure 1C), averaged across every country-election year in our data set (note that these figures display the overall average computed levels for each country.) For our difference-based measure, higher values on the horizontal axis denote higher (i.e., more intense) affective polarization levels. The Netherlands is by far the *least* affectively polarized country in our study: across the four Dutch CSES surveys (1998, 2002, 2006, 2010), the average computed affective polarization level, 2.94, denotes that on average Dutch partisans' (weighted) thermometer ratings of out-parties were less than 3

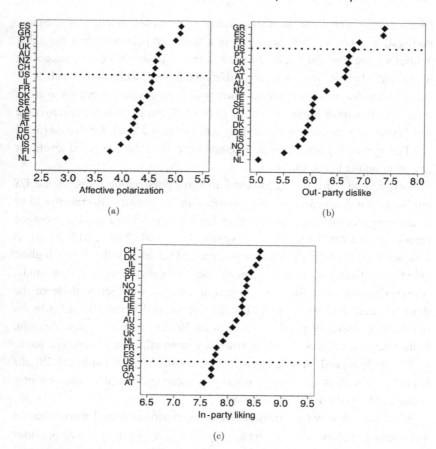

**Figure 1** Cross-national variations in affective polarization and its components

**Note:** Figure 1 presents aggregate country averages over the 1996–2017 period covered in our data. Figure 1A presents country-level affective polarization averages, where higher values on the x-axis denote higher levels of affective polarization. Figure 1B presents country-level averages for out-party dislike, where higher values on the x-axis denote more intense out-party dislike. Figure 1C presents country-level average of in-party liking; higher values on the x-axis denote higher in-party liking. In the three sub-figures, the dashed lines highlight values for the United States. Abbreviations are as follows. AU: Australia; AT: Austria; CA: Canada; DK: Denmark; FI: Finland; FR: France; DE: Germany; UK: Great Britain; GR: Greece; IS: Iceland; IE: Ireland; IL: Israel; NL: Netherlands; NZ: New Zealand; NO: Norway; PT: Portugal; ES: Spain; SE: Sweden; CH: Switzerland; US: United States.

units below their average in-party ratings, on the 0-to-10 thermometer scale. The second-least polarized public, Finland, has a difference-based affective polarization level of 3.78, nearly one unit higher (i.e., more intense) than the

Dutch public. The three Southern European countries in our study, Spain, Portugal, and Greece, appear far more affectively polarized than the other publics we analyze. For Spain, the most intensely polarized country according to our calculations, the computed difference-based polarization level, 5.09, denotes that Spanish respondents' ratings of their in-party were on average more than five units higher than their (weighted) out-party ratings, across the four Spanish CSES surveys in our study. The computed levels for Greece (5.06) and Portugal (4.99) are nearly as high and far exceed the computed levels for any other public in our study.

According to our differenced-based affective polarization measure, *the US public does not appear intensely polarized in comparative perspective*. The mean computed affective polarization level in the United States, averaged across the five American CSES surveys (1996, 2004, 2008, 2012, 2016), is 4.58 units on the 0-to-10 thermometer scale. This is only the eighth highest affective polarization average among the twenty countries in our study. America's computed affective polarization level is well below those of the three Southern European publics (Spain, Greece, and Portugal), and is in the middle of a cluster of publics that includes Britain, Australia, New Zealand, France, and Switzerland.[14] While America's mean affective polarization score, 4.58, slightly exceeds the average across our twenty Western publics (4.38), the United States does *not* appear unusually polarized, based on our country averages across the 1996–2017 period.

While readers may be surprised by our conclusion that the United States is not intensely polarized in comparative perspective, we note that in previous research across the same countries we analyze here, we cross-nationally compared affective polarization levels between the two largest parties on the left and right in each country, and again concluded that America's affective polarization level was near the average (and the median) among Western publics (Gidron et al. 2019a). This suggests that our conclusions about the US public are not driven by the presence of small, divisive parties in the multi-party systems found outside the United States: the US public appears unexceptional even in cross-national comparisons that are limited to partisans' feelings toward large, mainstream parties. At the same time, we emphasize that our comparisons here are of countries' *average* affective polarization

---

[14] Switzerland's surprisingly intense affective polarization level reflects the strength of the Swiss radical right and the high salience of issues related to national identity, such as European integration and immigration. Kriesi (2015, 725) notes, "By the 2000s, driven by the mobilization of the SVP [the radical right Swiss People's Party] against European integration and immigration, the Swiss party system had become more polarized than the corresponding systems of Germany, France, the UK, the Netherlands and Austria."

levels across the entire 1996–2017 period of our study. We present computations below suggesting that America's affective polarization has intensified in the two most recent presidential elections, 2012 and 2016.

While most extant affective polarization research is confined to the United States, our findings corroborate the limited comparative work on this topic. In one of the first such comparisons, Reiljan (2020) shows that "the level of AP [affective polarization] in the United States is actually exceeded by a number of democratic European countries," while Lauka et al. (2018, 117) locate the United States far from the top of their list of affectively polarized countries. Wagner (2020) develops several alternative affective polarization measures which all locate the United States near the midpoint among Western publics. The fact that these studies, employing different affective polarization measures, all reach the same substantive conclusion substantiates our finding about American non-exceptionalism in comparative perspective.

## 2.3 Cross-National Comparisons of Out-Party Dislike and In-Party Liking

Figure 1B displays country averages for out-party dislike, where higher values denote more intense dislike, while Figure 1C displays in-party evaluations for which higher values denote more positive (warmer) feelings toward the respondents' preferred party. We note first the greater cross-national variation in out-party dislike, compared to in-party liking. The national averages for out-party dislike range from a low value of 5.03 for The Netherlands, almost exactly at the neutral point (5) of the 0-to-10 thermometer scale, to a high (i.e., most intense) value of 7.36 for Greece, while the national averages for in-party liking vary only between 7.56 (Austria) to 8.60 (Switzerland). This reflects the fact that partisans almost invariably *like* their own party, so that the mean in-party liking scores all cluster at the warm end of the thermometer scale.

We now cross-nationally compare partisans' expressed in-party likes and out-party dislikes, while reminding readers that such comparisons may be problematic if publics differ in their interpretations of the party thermometer scale, or if there are cross-national differences in the social desirability of different party ratings. (This is why we privilege our difference-based affective polarization measure, which, as discussed previously, mitigates some of these problems.) Nevertheless, to the extent that cross-national comparisons of in-party liking and out-party dislike scores are meaningful, they suggest that American partisans feel less warmly toward political parties (both their own and its opponent) than do partisans in most Western publics. As displayed in Figure 1B, US partisans place fourth highest out of the twenty Western publics in the intensity of their expressed out-party dislike: the US mean out-party dislike score, 6.79 on the party thermometer scale (where 10 denotes maximum dislike), is well above the twenty-country average of 6.28. In this regard, the US public is in a cluster with the French, Canadian, Portuguese, British, and Australian publics, which all score between 6.7 and 6.9 on the out-party dislike scale; however these publics all appear much less hostile toward out-parties than do Spanish and Greek partisans, whose average out-party ratings are near 7.5 on the thermometer scale. With respect to in-party liking, American partisans express comparatively cool feelings toward their own party. As displayed in Figure 2C, American survey respondents' mean in-party thermometer rating was only 7.73, the fourth lowest among our twenty publics (exceeding only Austria, Canada, and Greece) and well below the twenty-country average of 8.13.

Overall, our comparisons suggest that American partisans display comparatively little warmth toward their in-party, and comparatively intense hostility toward its opponent – but that these feelings are not dramatic outliers among the twenty Western publics in our study. Note, moreover, that while US partisans' comparatively intense hostility toward opponents *intensifies* difference-based affective polarization, their comparative lack of warmth for their own party *defuses* affective polarization by narrowing the difference between their feelings toward their in-party and their put-party. This is why US partisans' evaluations of both their in- and out-parties are fairly distinct (though not exceptional) in comparative perspective, yet America's overall level of affective polarization – defined as the difference between their in-party and their out-party affect – lies near the midpoint across our twenty Western publics.

## 2.4 Cross-National Trends in Affective Polarization

We now shift our focus away from comparisons of within-country averages for affective polarization, to analyze *over-time trends* within countries across the 1996–2017 time period of our study. While previous studies analyze changes in American affective polarization over several decades (Iyengar et al. 2012, 2019; Mason 2018), we analyze the shorter 1996–2017 period covered by the CSES, for which we can compare the United States to most other Western publics.[15]

In analyzing affective polarization trends, we compare respondents' party ratings *in the same country* but at different time points.[16] Figure 2 displays, for

---

[15] See Boxell et al. (2020) for a comparative study that extends farther back in time but analyzes fewer countries.

[16] It seems plausible that within countries, survey respondents' interpretations of the party thermometer scale questions we analyze are reasonably stable across the period of our study – that is, that a US respondent's party rating of 6 (for instance) on the 0-to-10 thermometer scale has

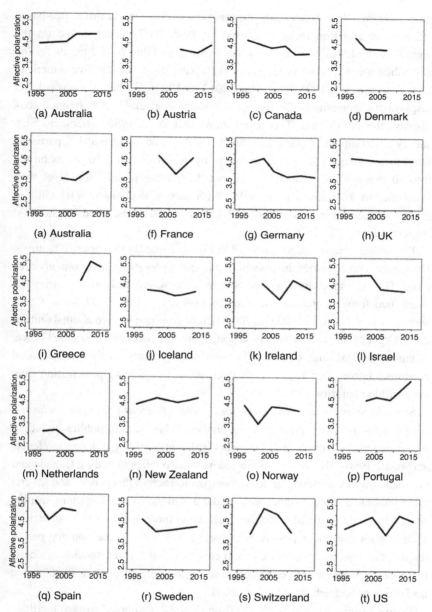

**Figure 2** Cross-national trends in affective polarization

**Note:** Figure 2 presents country-level trends in affective polarization, defined as the difference between survey respondents' thermometer ratings of their in-party versus their average ratings of out-parties. Higher values on the y-axis denote higher levels of affective polarization. The operationalization of the affective polarization measure is defined in the body of the text.

each Western public in our study, the temporal changes in our difference-based affective polarization measure across the 1996–2017 period, based on the eighty-one CSES election surveys listed earlier in Table 2. The trends for the US public are displayed in the lower right-hand panel, for the five American CSES surveys from 1996, 2004, 2008, 2012, and 2016,[17] where the vertical axis displays the computed affective polarization level and the horizontal axis displays the survey year. This panel shows that in the 1996 American CSES survey the computed polarization level was 4.30, denoting that US partisans rated their in-party above their-out-party by an average of 4.30 points on the 0-to-10 thermometer scale. The computed affective polarization level then intensifies to 4.90 units in the 2004 CSES survey, declines to 4.01 units in 2008, and then intensifies to 4.97 and 4.69 in the 2012 and 2016 US surveys, respectively.

The within-country trends pictured in Figure 2 display two notable features. First, in several countries the *affective polarization levels fluctuate sharply over time*. This is especially true for Switzerland, where affective polarization intensified from a computed level of about 4 units in the 1997 Swiss CSES survey to over 5 units in 2003 and 2007, before dropping back to about 4 units in 2011. Other countries that display striking temporal fluctuations include France, Ireland, Portugal, and Greece. The next section analyzes the political and economic factors that help explain fluctuations in affective polarization over time within countries.

Second, *there is no clear over time trend of intensifying (or declining) affective polarization across Western publics*. While several publics including the United States, Greece, and Portugal display intensifying polarization levels across the 1996–2017 period of our study, other publics including Canada and Germany display declining affective polarization across this period; and several other publics, notably Iceland, New Zealand, and the United Kingdom, display relatively stable levels of affective polarization (note however that our British sample does not cover post-Brexit elections). Finally, these country panels display the gaps in the CSES election coverage that we discussed previously: there are no Austrian or Greek election surveys included from before 2008, and no Danish or Spanish surveys after 2008.

Figure 3 summarizes the patterns from Figure 2, displayed so as to facilitate cross-national comparisons between the United States and other Western publics. In Figure 3A, the thick black line tracks trends in American affective

---

similar substantive interpretations in 1996 and in 2016, and that the same holds for other Western publics. Thus the within-country trends we analyze may not raise the same measurement issues as our cross-national comparisons of respondents' thermometer ratings.

[17] Recall that the CSES does not cover the 2000 US election.

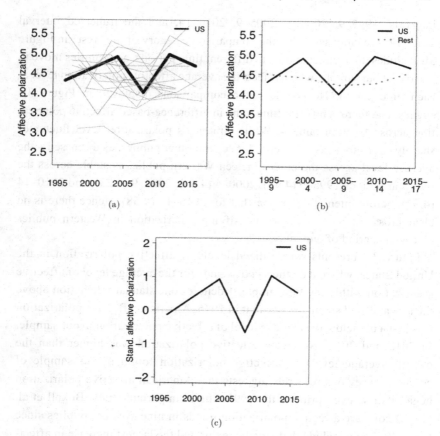

**Figure 3** American affective polarization in comparative perspective
**Note:** Figure 3 presents trends in American affective polarization in comparative perspective, defined as the difference between partisan respondents' in-party and their (weighted) out-party thermometer ratings. Higher values on the y-axis denote higher levels of affective polarization. In Figure 3A, the black line tracks trends in American affective polarization and the gray lines display trends in the other nineteen countries in our sample. In Figure 3B, the black line again displays trends in American affective polarization while the dashed gray line presents five-year averages of affective polarization in the other nineteen countries in our sample. Figure 3C presents standardized values of American affective polarization, where 0 denotes the average level of affective polarization and 1 denotes 1 standard deviation of affective polarization levels within the full sample.

polarization levels across the period of our study, while each of the nineteen gray lines traces trends in one of the other publics. Figure 3B displays affective polarization in the United States next to the average affective polarization level in these other nineteen Western publics, organized into five-year intervals: 1995–9, 2000–4, 2005–9, 2010–14, and the truncated interval 2015–17. We emphasize that the comparison category of the "rest" in Figure 3B includes different countries in different time periods, as countries move in and out of our sample, which affects the average affective polarization level in each time period. Nevertheless, the comparisons displayed in Figure 3B suggest that there is no clear time trend in difference-based affective polarization across Western publics. While America's polarization level fluctuates sharply over time – as is the case for several other publics, as discussed – the average level across the other nineteen Western publics is stable across the five year periods 1995–9 (4.49), 2000–4 (4.45), 2005–9 (4.23), and 2010–14 (4.32), before intensifying somewhat for 2015–17 (4.58). Hence there is no clear cross-national trend of intensifying polarization in Western publics across the period of our study.

Figure 3C presents standardized levels of affective polarization in the United States, where 0 on the y-axis stands for the average level of affective polarization within the full sample, 1 denotes one standard deviation above the average, and so on. We see that in 1996, American affective polarization was just a bit below the average level of affective polarization in our sample. In 2012 and 2016, American affective polarization was higher than the overall average levels of affective polarization found in our sample of countries. Previous research suggests that American affective polarization began its rise even prior to the 1990s. In an important study, Boxell et al. (2020) compare affective polarization trends in nine Western publics since the 1980s and conclude that "the US exhibited the largest increase in affective polarization over this period" (p. 2), showing that the rate of increase in affective polarization was stronger in the United States than in other Western publics before the mid 1990s. In summary, these findings suggest that American affective polarization – although still not exceptional – has intensified more than in most Western publics since 1996.

## 2.5 Cross-National Trends in Out-Party Dislike and In-Party Liking

We next consider cross-national trends in the two components of difference-based affective polarization: out-party dislike and in-party liking. Previous studies conclude that it is US partisans' intensifying dislike of out-parties, not changes in their in-party liking, that drive growing difference-based affective polarization (Iyengar et al. 2012, 2019). Yet, to date, no cross-national study assesses whether intensifying out-party dislike is a general feature across Western publics.

Figure 4 displays the temporal trends in our out-party dislike measure in each public in our study, again based on the eighty-one CSES surveys across the 1996–2017 period. Here, the vertical axis in each country panel displays the computed out-party dislike level, where higher numbers denote more intense out-party dislike. The horizontal axis again displays the survey year. The lower right-hand panel shows that US partisans' computed levels of out-party dislike intensified from a mean value of 6.50 in 1996 to 6.88 in 2004, along the 0-to-10 thermometer scale;[18] that out-party dislike then declined to 6.34 in 2008; and that US partisans' mean out-party dislike subsequently intensified sharply, to 7.00 in 2012 and then to 7.25 in 2016. The 2016 level is nearly a full unit higher than that from eight years earlier (6.34 in 2008) and is the most intense out-party dislike recorded for the United States across the 1996–2016 period – results that are in line with previous research documenting Americans' intensifying out-party dislike. This is consistent with research suggesting that American politics became more divisive under President Obama, in part fueled by large of a growing cleavage over racial issues and questions of national identity (Sides et al. 2018; Tesler 2016), a hypothesis we substantiate in Section 3.

The computations displayed in Figure 4 suggest that several publics, including Ireland, Greece, and Portugal mirror the United States in displaying significant over-time increases in out-party dislike; indeed Ireland, Greece, and Portugal all feature sharper over-time increases than the United States, at least when comparing levels in the earliest versus the most recent CSES survey in each country. However other publics, including Canada, Denmark, and Germany, display declines in out-party dislike, while Finland, France, the UK, Iceland, Israel, New Zealand, and Sweden display temporally stable patterns.[19]

Figure 5 summarizes the patterns from Figure 4, displayed to facilitate cross-national comparisons of the United States versus other Western publics. Figure 5A tracks trends in American out-party dislike (the thick black line) across the period of our study, while each gray line traces trends in one of the other nineteen publics. Figure 5B displays out-party dislike in the United States next to the average out-party dislike in the other nineteen publics in our study, again organized into the time intervals 1995–9, 2000–4, 2005–9, 2010–14, and 2015–17. The comparisons in Figure 5B suggest that, notwithstanding the temporal variations across publics discussed previously, *there is an overall trend of intensifying out-party dislike over the past several years, both in the United States and across Western publics as a whole.*

---

[18] Recall again that the 2000 US election is missing from the CSES.

[19] The CSES has not yet released recent election surveys from the UK (2017 and 2019) and Israel (2015, 2019, and 2020), where popular accounts suggest that out-party dislike intensified.

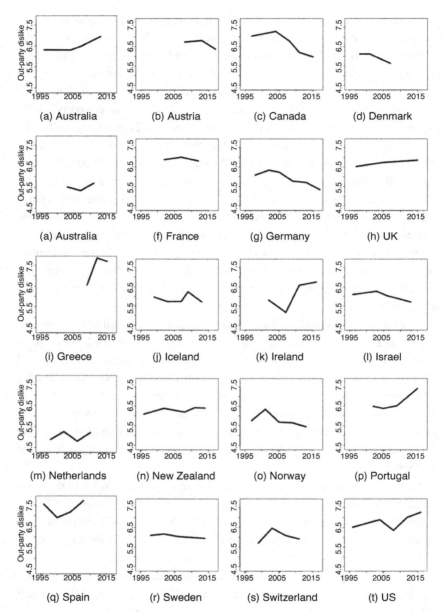

**Figure 4** Cross-national trends in out-party dislike

**Note:** Figure 4 presents country-level trends in out-party dislike. Higher values on the y-axis denote more intense out-party dislike. The operationalization of out-party dislike is defined in the body of the text.

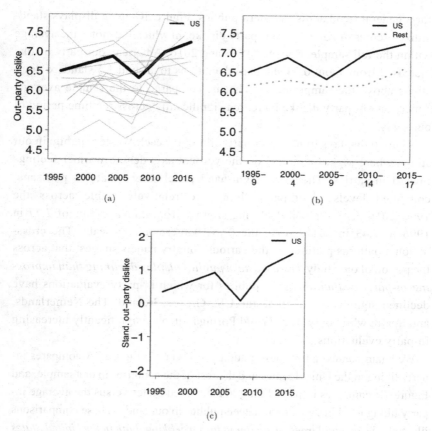

**Figure 5** American out-party dislike in comparative perspective
**Note:** Figure 5 presents trends in American out-party dislike in comparative perspective, where higher values on the y-axis denote more intense out-party dislike. In Figure 5A, the black line displays trends in American out-party dislike and the gray lines show trends in out-party dislike in the other nineteen publics in our sample. In Figure 5B, the black line displays trends in American out-party dislike and the dashed gray line presents 5-year averages of out-party dislike in the other nineteen Western publics. Figure 5 C presents standardized values of American out-party dislike, where 0 denotes the average level of affective polarization and 1 denotes 1 standard deviation of affective polarization levels within the full sample.

The computations displayed in Figure 5B suggest that the mean out-party dislike level across the nineteen non-US publics in our study was relatively stable across the 1995–2014 period (based on the five-year averages) but intensified in the most recent time period. Yet since we only have a limited number of cases for this 2015–17 time period (eight cases including the United States), we caution against interpreting this as convincing evidence for a general trend across Western publics. Figure 5C again displays standardized scores of American out-party dislike, in which 0 denotes the average within the full sample. Between 1996 and 2016, American out-party dislike increased from about 0.34 standard deviations to around 1.5 standard deviations above the sample mean. That is, compared to the sample average, American out-party dislike increased significantly across the time period of our study.

Figure 6 displays trends in in-party liking for each Western public in our study, where higher numbers on the vertical axis denote warmer feelings toward in-parties. The lower right-hand panel shows that US partisans' computed levels of in-party liking are relatively stable across the 1996–2016 period, albeit declining slightly from a mean value of 7.77 in 1996 to 7.43 in 2016, along the 0-to-10 thermometer scale. The cross-national patterns pictured in the various country panels suggest that across the period of our study, *more Western publics display declining than improving in-party evaluations.* The publics for which in-party evaluations have declined significantly include the UK, Greece, Ireland, The Netherlands, and Spain, while only Austria and Portugal display significantly increasing in-party evaluations.

We again contextualize these findings in Figure 7. Figure 7A compares in-party liking in the United States and the rest of the countries in our sample, and Figure 7B compares in-party liking in the United States versus the average in-party liking level in the other nineteen publics in our study. These comparisons illustrate the *gradual trend of declining in-party liking, both in the United States and across Western publics as a whole, on average.* The mean in-party liking level across the nineteen non-US publics declines gradually yet consistently across time periods: from 8.34 for 1995–99, to 8.18 for 2000–4, to 8.11 for 2005–9, to 8.09 for 2010–14, and to 8.01 for 2015–17. Figure 7C presents the standardized values of American in-party liking, which declined from about 0.8 standard deviations below the mean in 1996 to more than 1.6 standard deviation below the sample mean in 2016.

To summarize what we have found so far: while average levels of American affective polarization are not intense in comparative perspective, dislike toward partisan opponents did increase rather sharply in the United States between 1996 and 2016 – more so than in most other Western democracies. Put differently, *the United States is not an outlier in terms of levels of affective polarization, but it does stand out when we focus on changes in out-party dislike since the mid 1990s.* Between 1996 and 2016, Americans have come to more strongly dislike their partisan opponents while adopting somewhat cooler feelings toward their own parties.

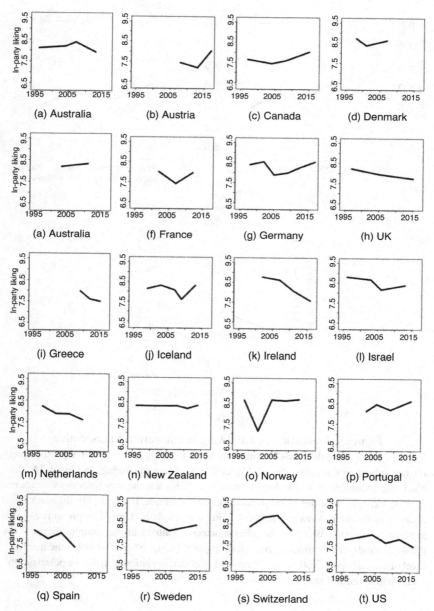

**Figure 6** Cross-national trends in in-party liking

**Note:** Figure 6 presents country-level trends in in-party liking. Higher values on the y-axis denote higher levels of in-party liking. The operationalization of in-party liking is defined in the body of the text.

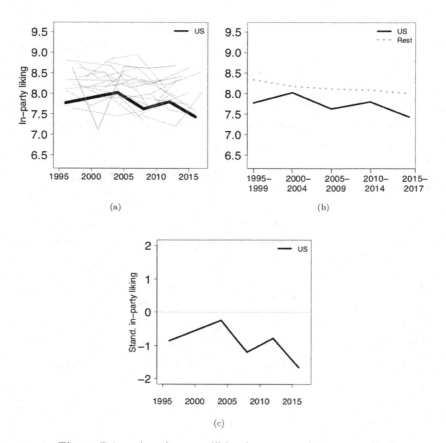

**Figure 7** American in-party liking in comparative perspective

**Note:** Figure 7 presents trends in American in-party liking in comparative perspective. Higher values on the y-axis denote higher levels of in-party liking. In Figure 7A, the black line documents trends in American in-party liking and the gray lines show trends in in-party liking in the other nineteen countries in our sample. In Figure 7B, the black line documents trends in American in-party liking and the dashed gray line presents 5-year averages of in-party liking in the other nineteen countries in our sample. Figure 7 C presents standardized values of American in-party liking, where 0 denotes the average level of affective polarization and 1 denotes 1 standard deviation of affective polarization levels within the full sample.

## 2.6 Conclusions: Do Not Exaggerate American Affective Polarization, Do Be Concerned about Its Rise

This section provided a panoramic view of affective polarization in the United States and other Western democracies since the mid 1990s. We have applied our comparative strategy to analyze affective polarization across twenty Western publics between 1996 and 2017, a period for which the CSES includes common survey items measuring citizens' partisanship and their party thermometer ratings. While inter-party hostility, distrust, and contempt are disturbing features of many contemporary polities, most extant research addresses the American case in isolation. Our goal in this section was to situate the United States in a comparative context, in order to examine how levels of and changes in American affective polarization compare to those in other Western polities.

We highlight two main observations about American affective polarization in comparative perspective. On the one hand, our finding that the United States is not unduly affectively polarized in cross-national perspective may comfort observers who are dismayed by the intense inter-party hostility, scorn, and distrust in contemporary American politics: several other Western polities appear equally (or even more intensely) affectively polarized. This is not to say we should not be concerned about fractures in the American social fabric caused by intense animosity across partisan lines; but it does suggest we should not exaggerate America's political divisions compared to other Western countries. A flipside of this finding is that, to the extent we worry that affective polarization undermines American politics, the citizens in several other Western publics may have reason to be equally concerned about the comparatively intense political divisions in their countries.

On the other hand, dislike of out-parties did increase more sharply in the United States compared to most other Western democracies across the period of our study, and we have seen that by the times of the 2012 and 2016 presidential elections, Americans' expressed hostility toward out-parties was among the more intense computed levels of out-party dislike across the eighty-one election surveys in our twenty-country study. The rise in Americans' dislike of the opposing party has been documented in previous work, which extends deeper in time (Abramowitz and Webster 2016; Boxell 2020; Iyengar et al. 2012). The value of our comparative approach lies in the observation that Americans' out-party hostility has increased more sharply than what we see in most other Western democracies (although there is suggestive evidence that growing out-party dislike may be a cross-national trend). In the next section we will examine several factors that can help explain such cross-national and over-time variations in affective polarization.

## 3 Explaining Variations in Affective Polarization in the United States and Abroad

In Section 2, we showed that affective polarization in mass publics, defined as the degree to which partisans prefer their own party to its opponents, varies both across and within Western publics. We showed that, over the last twenty-five years, American affective polarization has not been exceptional in comparative perspective, but that American dislike of out-parties has intensified over this period.

In this section, we move beyond documenting cross-national and temporal affective polarization patterns, and consider explanations for when and where affective polarization intensifies. We analyze three country-level factors that scholars have linked to affective polarization: party elites' disagreements over ideology and policy; economic conditions, namely income inequality and unemployment; and countries' national electoral laws. The Western democracies we study feature widely different electoral laws, but these laws are stable within countries across the time period of our study (1996–2017). Similarly, income inequality varies sharply between Western democracies, but changes rather slowly over time within these countries. Electoral laws and income inequality, therefore, lend themselves to *cross-national comparisons*. By contrast, unemployment and party elites' ideological and policy disputes evolve substantially over time within countries, so we can analyze whether within-country changes in these variables predict changes in affective polarization.

We first review previous scholarship linking elite policy disputes, national economic conditions, and electoral laws to affective polarization in Western publics. We then empirically evaluate these links by estimating multivariate regression models, which predict the intensity of affective polarization in a given country-election year as a function of the country's levels of income inequality and unemployment, its electoral laws, and the intensity of party elites' policy disagreements. This multivariate approach allows us to estimate the relationship between the intensity of affective polarization in given country-election year and the level of each explanatory variable, while holding other explanatory factors constant. We can thus answer questions such as: "All else equal (namely unemployment, elite policy disagreements, and electoral laws), are higher levels of income inequality associated with more intense levels of affective polarization? And, what is the strength of this relationship?"

We report four empirical findings. First, we estimate that affective polarization is more intense in countries with greater income inequality, all else equal, a finding with implications for the United States, which is the most economically *unequal* Western democracy in our study. Second, we estimate that within countries, affective polarization intensifies over time as unemployment rises, all else equal. This finding is notable because the United States enjoyed relatively low unemployment across much of the 1996–2017 time period of our study – yet this finding has troubling implications for the present and (possibly) the future, given the current unemployment spike in response to the coronavirus health crisis, which may intensify affective polarization in the United States (and abroad), especially if the current economic recession across Western democracies is prolonged. Third, we estimate that, all else equal, affective polarization intensifies over time within countries as party elites disagree more sharply on cultural issues such as multiculturalism, law and order, and the national way of life; by contrast, we detect no relationship between affective polarization and the intensity of elites' economic disagreements. These findings are notable because US Democratic and Republican elites have polarized more sharply on cultural issues over the past twenty-five years than have the elites in any other Western party system, according to our measures. These findings differ from research emphasizing the relationship between American elites' economic polarization and mass-level affective polarization (Abramowitz and Webster 2017). Finally, we estimate that, holding other factors constant, countries that employ winner-take-all, first-past-the-post voting systems to select their representations – such as the United States, Canada, and France – display more intense out-party dislike than do the countries that employ more proportional voting systems.

There are arguments both for and against drawing causal inferences from the statistical relationships we estimate; that is, the inference that income inequality, high unemployment, party elites' cultural disputes, and single-winner voting systems *cause* affective polarization to intensify within mass publics. In particular, we urge caution in ascribing causal effects to income inequality and electoral laws – the factors we analyze that vary mostly *between* countries but not *within* countries over time – because we recognize that countries differ across many dimensions (including geography, culture, social institutions, media regimes, and their democratic histories) that we cannot fully account for in our cross-national comparisons. At the same time, the relationships we estimate support theoretical arguments advanced in previous studies, that income inequality and electoral rules drive affective polarization. By contrast, we feel more confident in inferring that higher unemployment rates and elite cultural disagreements cause affective polarization, since these factors co-vary within countries over time and moreover as we discuss below there are strong theoretical reasons to expect these relationships. Overall, our empirical analyses provide a prima facie case that all of the factors we analyze help explain variations in affective polarization – although we do not claim to have conclusively established these causal relationships. Our analyses thereby suggest that America's comparatively high income inequality, intense elite cultural disputes, and single-winner voting system all intensify affective polarization in the mass public, but that America's comparatively low unemployment rate over much of the past twenty-five years has defused affective polarization.

We first review previous research linking affective polarization to elite ideological and policy polarization, economic conditions, and electoral institutions. We then describe our variable measures, and we report multivariate regression analyses linking these factors to affective polarization levels in Western democracies. We then discuss how our analyses illuminate American affective polarization, both cross-nationally and over time.

## 3.1 Explaining Variations in Affective Polarization

### 3.1.1 The Role of Elite Ideological and Policy Disagreements

American politics scholars have debated whether and how political elites' ideological and policy disagreements can drive partisan hostility toward political opponents. Elite-level ideological polarization in the United States has increased since in the 1970s, as Democratic and Republican politicians have sharply diverged from each other with respect to their policy behavior. Analyses of roll-call votes in Congress show that "Congress is now more polarized than at any time since the end of Reconstruction" (Hare et al. 2014; see also Bonica 2014; McCarty et al. 2006; Pierson and Schickler 2020). This elite-level ideological polarization has been visible to the US public: Hetherington (2009) documents that survey respondents' party placements have increasingly diverged since the 1970s, with citizens ascribing increasingly conservative positions to the Republican Party and more liberal positions to the Democrats.

Some scholars argue that elite ideological polarization and mass-level affective polarization are linked (Abramowitz and Webster 2017; more broadly on policy disagreements, see Lelkes 2019; Orr and Huber 2020). Rogowski and Sutherland (2015), for instance, report experimental findings that stronger ideological differences between American candidates and officeholders drive affective polarization among citizens. Carlin and Love (2018) draw on social psychology research to explain the mechanism: when partisans view their opponents as opposing their core beliefs, they ascribe negative traits and direct negative emotions toward the other party. Zakharova and Warwick (2014) report cross-national analyses of surveys from fourteen democracies demonstrating that citizens ascribe more negative character traits to parties with whom they have ideological disagreements. Also examining this issue comparatively, Reiljan (2020) documents cross-national correlations between elite ideological polarization on the left–right dimension, and the intensity of affective polarization in the mass public.

Other scholars, however, question the direct relationship between ideological and affective polarization (Lelkes 2019 reviews this debate). Mason (2018) suggests that affective polarization in the US public is primarily driven by the growing overlap of citizens' religious, racial, and partisan identities, not ideology (see Huddy et al. 2018 for a related argument in the European context). From this standpoint, rival parties' partisans may share similar policy stands, or lack coherent policy preferences (Kinder and Kalmoe 2017), but still dislike their political opponents – or, as Mason (2015) cleverly noted, opposing partisans may "disrespectfully agree." The studies summarized above motivate our first hypothesis:

*H1a (The elite ideological polarization hypothesis). Ideological polarization between rival parties' elites intensifies mass-level affective polarization.*

*The differential effects of elite disputes on economics versus cultural issues: The cultural primacy hypothesis.* While political commentators often frame policy disputes in terms of the liberal-conservative (or left–right) dimension, the ideological space across Western democracies comprises at least two distinct sub-dimensions: an *economic dimension* pertaining to income redistribution and the scope of state intervention in the economy, and a *cultural dimension* that relates to issues of national identity and multiculturalism (Ellis and Stimson 2012; Hooghe and Marks 2018; Kitschelt 1994; Kriesi et al. 2008).[20] And there are reasons to expect elite cultural disagreements, more than economic debates, to drive affective polarization in the mass public.

Elite disputes on cultural issues, broadly defined to encompass questions of national identity, multiculturalism, and moral values, might generate especially intense political hostility. While people may compromise over economic issues, it is harder to compromise on cultural issues that are intertwined with deeply held beliefs about religion, race, or national identity (Goren and Chapp 2017). Tavits (2007) highlights this distinction between 'principled' issues such as national identity on which citizens reject elite compromise, and 'pragmatic' issues such as economic policies on which citizens may approve of elite flexibility. Even in the 1970s, Converse and Markus (1979) speculated that "moral issues have 'deeper resonance' and are more 'crystallized' than opinions on fiscal and foreign policy issues" (cited in Goren and Chapp 2017, 112). Norris and Inglehart (2019, 54) similarly note that "Economic issues are characteristically incremental, allowing left and right-wing parties to bargain and compromise . . . By contrast, cultural issues, and the politicization of social identities, tend to divide into 'Us-versus-Them' tribes, bringing uncompromising and extreme party polarization." As

---

[20] We follow an extensive literature that distinguishes between the economic and cultural dimensions of Western politics. That being said, we recognize that there are issues – such as European integration – that carry both cultural and economic implications, and that these dimensions interact in shaping people's worldviews (Cramer 2016; Gidron and Hall 2017, 2020).

Sides et al. (2018, p. 10; emphasis added) note in the context of the US 2016 election:

> Issues like immigration, racial discrimination, and the integration of Muslims boil down to competing visions of American identity and inclusiveness. To have politics oriented around this debate – as opposed to more prosaic issues like, say, entitlement reform – makes politics *"feel"* angrier, precisely because debates about ethnic, racial, and national identities engender strong emotions.

American politics research links intensifying elite cultural disputes with mass-level affective polarization. Hetherington et al. (2016) show that mass polarization in American society is linked to moral and racial issues. Skocpol and Williamson (2011) also highlight concerns over cultural decline and the changing racial landscape as one root cause of the anger that made the Tea Party a potent force within the Republican Party. Cultural worldviews relating to nationalism and race increasingly define the electoral bases of the Democratic and Republican parties (Bonikowski et al. 2019; Hetherington and Weiler 2018), which Drutman argues has intensified affective polarization: "elevation of *culture-war politics*, more than anything else, created the distinct and charged divisions that now define the two-party coalitions. This divide is driving the toxic politics of today" (Drutman 2019). Along similar lines, Levitsky and Ziblatt (2018, 171; emphases added) contend that "the two [American] parties are now *divided over race and religion* – two deeply polarizing issues that tend to generate *greater intolerance and hostility* than traditional policy issues such as taxes and government."

Other Western democracies also feature growing elite cultural disputes, although below we show that the culture wars have intensified especially sharply in the United States. Since the 1980s, citizens across Western democracies increasingly define their political identities based on cultural worldviews (de Vries et al. 2013), while party elites increasingly emphasize culture at the expense of economic issues such as welfare, taxation, and redistribution (Hall 2020). As described by Norris and Inglehart (2019, 50; emphasis added):

> [T]oday *the most heated political issues in Western societies are cultural*, dealing with the integration of ethnic minorities, immigration, and border control, Islamic-related terrorism, same-sex marriage and LGBTQ rights, divisions over the importance of national sovereignty versus international cooperation, the provision of development aid, the deployment of nuclear weapons, and issues of environmental protection and climate change.

Perhaps surprisingly, cultural issues continued to grow in salience even during the global financial crisis beginning in 2009 (Hutter et al. 2019; Sides et al.

2018), when economic hardship was often interpreted through a cultural lens, and linked with national identity, rural-vs-urban cultural worldviews, and race (Cramer 2016).

In contrast to the reasoning outlined above, other scholars link intensifying American affective polarization to economic debates, not culture. Abramowitz and Webster (2017, 633) and Iyengar et al. (2012, 422) both find that affective polarization in the United States correlates more strongly with attitudes on economic policy than with cultural disputes over issues such as gay rights. However, we note that gay rights is an issue on which partisans of *both* major American parties have shifted left, and thus may not drive affective polarization in the same way as immigration and racial debates, on which the Democratic and Republican partisan constituencies have diverged (Bonikowski et al. 2019). Moreover, scholars note the analytical challenge of separating the racial component of some economic policy debates. For example, welfare policy is clearly an economic issue, yet scholars find that Americans' racial attitudes predict attitudes toward welfare because the public views the policy as aiding racial and ethnic minorities (Gilens 1999). These considerations prompt the following hypothesis:

*H1b (The cultural primacy hypothesis). Affective polarization in mass publics intensifies more in response to elite disputes over cultural issues than over economic issues.*

### 3.1.2 National Economic Conditions: Inequality and Unemployment

Previous research links economic inequality with elite-level ideological disagreements (McCarty 2019, 78–81). McCarty et al. (2006) demonstrate that American economic inequality correlates with elite ideological polarization: both were high in the early twentieth century, then dropped in the 1930s and remained low for about forty years, before they began climbing together beginning in the 1970s (see also Mickey et al. 2017). This relationship also holds sub-nationally: examining American state legislatures, Voorheis et al. (2015) find that economic inequality intensifies elite ideological polarization.

We might expect economic inequality to be associated not only with elite ideological polarization, but also with mass-level affective polarization. Levitsky and Ziblatt (2018, 228–229) suggest that reducing inequality could decrease affective polarization in the United States, while Drutman (2019, 145) similarly argues that "when inequality continues to increase, more resentment follows." In a comparative overview of polarization, McCoy and Somer (2019,

241) contend that higher economic inequality opens the door for "pernicious polarization," as it increases the resonance of polarizing messages among those who feel left behind by economic inequality. In one of the only systematic empirical investigations of this issue, Stewart et al. (2020) uncover a strong relationship between affective polarization and economic inequality across the American states. Hitlin and Harkness (2017, chapter 6) outline a potential causal mechanism, arguing that economic inequality "begets negative moral emotions," and is socially divisive because it prompts envy toward the top and scorn toward those at the bottom. These considerations support the hypothesis:

*H2a (The income inequality hypothesis). Income inequality intensifies affective polarization, in analyses that control for elite-level ideological polarization.*

Scholars highlight other economic conditions that may intensify affective polarization, including a relationship between weaker national economic conditions and declining political trust and satisfaction with democracy (Clarke et al. 1993; Gilley 2006) – attitudes that may connect to partisans' dislike for out-parties. There is also evidence that economic downturns prompt the rise of radical populist parties (Funke et al. 2016; Hobolt and Tilley 2016), which are usually strongly disliked by mainstream partisans (Gidron et al. 2019b; Helbling and Jungkunz 2020; Mudde and Kaltwasser 2018).

Unemployment is a key feature of economic downturns that is highly visible to mass publics (more so than changes in GDP, for instance), and has been connected to rising levels of polarization in American politics (Lopez and Ramirez 2004). Across the Atlantic, research concludes that the global financial crisis beginning in 2008, and the rising unemployment that followed, prompted more adversarial election campaigns (Kriesi and Hutter 2019), which are likely to intensify affective polarization in mass publics. These considerations motivate the hypothesis:

*H2b (The unemployment hypothesis). Unemployment intensifies affective polarization, in analyses that control for elite-level ideological polarization.*

### 3.1.3 Electoral Institutions

Finally, we posit a relationship between affective polarization and electoral rules. We distinguish between majoritarian political institutions such as disproportional, plurality-based voting systems that concentrate policy-making into the hands of a single party – one that often lacks majority popular support – versus consensual institutions with proportional voting systems that disperse policy-making authority among multiple parties that collectively enjoy broader support.[21] Lijphart (2010) argues and presents empirical evidence that the publics in the "kinder, gentler" consensual systems are more satisfied with democracy, while Anderson and Guillory (1997) show that democratic satisfaction expressed by supporters of "winning" versus "losing" parties are more similar in consensual systems. In related research, McCoy and Somer (2019, 261) analyze eleven polarized countries and conclude that the most extreme cases of polarization "emerge in contexts of majoritarian electoral systems that produce a disproportionate representation of the majority or plurality party." Majoritarian systems, they argue, generate an "us-versus-them" zero-sum politics that prompts increasing ideological and affective polarization.

Recent research ascribes America's intense affective polarization to its two-party system, which is sustained in part by the US plurality voting system.[22] Drutman (2019, 213) contrasts the polarizing dynamics of the US two-party system with the depolarizing dynamics of multiparty systems, which encourage compromise and cooperation across party lines, because parties need to form and maintain governing coalitions; by contrast, "toxic two-party politics creates a uniquely fertile ground for negative campaigning to spiral out of control, leaving resentful, distrustful voters in its wake." These considerations motivate our final hypothesis:

*H3 (The majoritarian institutions hypothesis). Affective polarization is more intense in countries with more majoritarian political institutions.*

## 3.2 Data and Measurement

We evaluate our hypotheses by empirically analyzing the relationship between affective polarization and our explanatory factors: elite ideological and policy polarization; national economic conditions, namely income inequality and unemployment; and electoral rules. Our affective polarization measure for a given country-year is the one we introduced in Section 2, namely the difference between survey respondents' mean ratings of their preferred party and their (weighted) average ratings of all other parties in the system on the 0-to-10

---

[21] The distinction between majoritarian and consensual institutions rests on additional factors besides electoral systems including federalism, executive-legislative relations, and interest group pluralism. The British "Westminster" system is the archetype majoritarian democracy, while the Netherlands and Switzerland are archetypical consensual democracies. In Appendix 3.4 (online) we report robustness checks using a measure of majoritarian/consensual institutions that accounts for these additional factors, which support the same substantive conclusions as our electoral systems analyses.

[22] Extensive research documents that countries with plurality voting systems tend to feature fewer major political parties than countries with proportional representation, all else equal, although plurality-based countries usually feature more than two major parties. See Taagepera and Shugart (1989) for a review of the theory and empirics underpinning this relationship.

thermometer scale, averaged across all respondents from the country-election survey year who reported a party identification. The set of eighty-one election surveys we analyze are those listed earlier in Table 2.

For data on party elite ideological and policy polarization we rely on the Comparative Manifesto Project (CMP) content analyses of parties' election manifestos, which parties in Western democracies publish in the run-up to national election campaigns. These documents, which Americans typically label *party platforms*, provide lengthy discussions of parties' issue positions and priorities. Given the extensive media coverage of these documents, they provide valuable snapshots of party elites' policy positions/emphases, as these messages are conveyed to the mass public around the time of the general election. The CMP codings have been used as measures of party elites' positions and emphases in hundreds of scholarly studies (for reviews see, e.g., Adams 2012; Volkens et al. 2017). Scholars have also validated the CMP scores against other measures of elite ideological polarization, and these scores provide face validity to the CMP measures (Adams et al. 2019; Bakker et al. 2015).

We first consider elite polarization on the left–right (or liberal–conservative) dimension. The Comparative Manifesto Project (CMP) codes the Left-Right tones of parties' election manifestos based on a fifty-six-category scheme, to derive an overall left–right score (RILE) for each party in each election year. Since these manifestos are approved by the party's leadership, we take the CMP Left-Right codings as our measure of the stated position of each party's elites. The logic underlying the CMP coding rules is that parties take positions by staking out opposing stands on specific policy debates (such as expanding versus limiting the welfare state, supporting versus opposing traditional morality, and so on), and also by emphasizing the importance of certain policy areas compared to others; for instance, leftist parties tend to emphasize social justice and environmental protection, while right-wing parties tend to emphasize crime and national defense. The coding procedure involves coding quasi-sentences in the manifesto, and then combining these codings to produce an overall Left-Right "tone" for each party's manifesto along a $-100$ to $+100$ scale where higher numbers denote a more right-wing tone. By applying this approach to all the major parties' manifestos in a country for a given election year, one can create a Left-Right 'mapping' of the party system. Appendix 3.1 in the online supplementary information memo provides full details of the CMP coding procedures.

We also analyze elite polarization on two specific policy dimensions: an *economic dimension* that captures state intervention in the economy, and a *cultural dimension* pertaining to issues of national identity and multiculturalism. Both the economic and cultural issue scales are derived from fifteen Comparative Manifesto Project (CMP) coding categories,[23] where the economic dimension is constructed based on the mixture of the party's positive versus negative references to welfare state expansion, invocations of Keynesian economic policies versus free-market capitalism, and so on, and the cultural dimension is constructed based on the mixture of positive versus negative references to multiculturalism, the national way of life, internationalism, and so on.

Our measure of overall elite party system polarization on each dimension (Left–Right, economic, or cultural) in a given election year is the dispersion (spread) of the CMP codings of the parties' positions on the relevant dimension in that year, weighted by each party's size. Intuitively, our measure is similar to our measure for affective polarization. For each pair of parties in the electoral system, we calculate the ideological distance between the two parties, and then weight this distance by party vote share. Our measure can be interpreted as the expected policy difference between two parties in a system if we drew two parties, without replacement, at random, weighted by each party's vote share. Full technical details of this calculation can be found in Appendix 3.2. Intuitively, in the US two-party system this measure is simply the absolute difference of the CMP codings of the Democratic and Republican parties' positions. For the multiparty systems found outside the United States, the polarization measure weights position differences between larger parties more heavily than differences between smaller, less electorally relevant, parties.

Figure 8 presents the standardized measures of elite left–right (panel a), economic (panel b), and cultural (panel c) polarization in the United States (the thin black line) and the other nineteen party systems in our sample (the light grey lines), over the time period 1996–2017. These scores are standardized, so that the 0 value on the y-axis denotes the average level of elite polarization within the overall sample. With respect to elite left–right ideological polarization, the United States has shifted from one standard deviation *below* the mean in 1996 to more than 1.5 standard deviations *above* the mean by 2016; that is, American left-right elite polarization was below the sample average in the mid 1990s but well above the average by 2016.

On economic policies (panel b), we also see increasing American elite polarization: from nearly one standard deviation below the mean in 1996 to about one standard deviation above the mean in 2016. The lowest level of elite economic polarization in our data set was measured in the United Kingdom in

---

[23] We note that the CMP team chose which categories to use to construct each dimension.

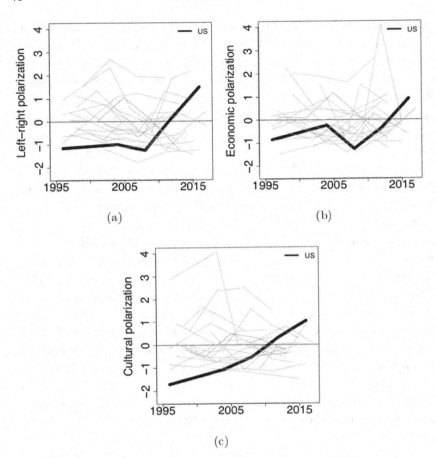

**Figure 8** American ideological polarization in comparative perspective

**Note:** Figure 8 presents trends in American elite polarization in comparative perspective. Higher values on the y-axis denote more intense polarization. The values on the y-axis are standardized, meaning that zero denotes the sample average. Figure 8A, Figure 8B and Figure 8 C present trends in left-right, economic and cultural elite polarization respectively. In all three figures, the black line represents trends in American elites' polarization and the gray lines show polarization trends in the other nineteen party systems in our sample.

1997, following the adoption of the Labour Party's moderate "Third Way" politics under its new leader Tony Blair, which shifted Labour sharply toward the center. The highest elite economic polarization level was recorded in Greece in 2012, following the financial crisis that transformed the Greek party system and prompted the rise of the populist, far left Syriza. We will discuss the Greek case when considering how the global economic crisis beginning in 2008 influenced affective polarization in Western democracies.

Panel c displays fluctuations in elite cultural polarization, showing that it is on this dimension that American elites have polarized most sharply over time. In 1996, the Democratic and Republican platforms converged with respect to their stated positions on cultural issues, according to the CMP codings: in fact, the 1996 US election features the *lowest* measured level of party elite cultural polarization among the eighty-one elections across the twenty Western party systems in our data set (it is located nearly two standard deviations below the sample average of elite cultural polarization). Yet by 2016 – the year when Republican presidential nominee Donald Trump centered his campaign on opposition to immigration and appeals to "Make America Great Again" – American elite cultural polarization had intensified to a level more than one standard deviation *above* the sample mean. American elites' cultural shift, from being the least polarized party system in our study in 1996 to one of the more polarized systems by 2016, represents the most dramatic elite cultural polarization increase among the twenty Western party systems in our study. At the same time, other party systems, including Israel and Switzerland, have displayed more intense elite cultural polarization than the United States in 2016.

Finally, the patterns in Figure 8 illustrate that while elite polarization on ideology, economics, and culture varies *between* countries, it also varies sharply *within* countries over time, not only for American elites (who have polarized over time along all three dimensions) but also for many other party systems in our study (whose polarization levels are tracked by the light grey lines). This is important because, as we will discuss, it will allow us to track whether elite ideological and policy polarization co-vary with mass-level affective polarization within countries over time.

With respect to economic conditions, we measure income inequality using Gini coefficient values from the Standardized World Income Inequality Database (SWIID version 8.2). A Gini coefficient of 0 denotes perfect equality (i.e., all incomes are equal) while 100 denotes maximum inequality (all income held by one individual) (Solt 2016). Unemployment data are from the World Bank. We note that the United States stands out on both economic indicators: the United States features the highest income inequality level among the twenty countries in our study (with a Gini coefficient of 38.2 in 2016, the highest country-year in our data set) but below-average unemployment rates (4.5 percent in 2016 and about 6 percent across the 1996–2017 period of our study, well below the average of 7.4 percent in our data set). The lowest income inequality level across the elections we analyze is for Denmark in 1998 (22.2); the lowest unemployment level is for Iceland in 2002 (2.2 percent) while the highest is for Greece in 2012 (24.4 percent). Finally, while income inequality varies sharply *between* countries (as between the United States and Denmark) it changes very slowly over time *within* countries across the 1996–2017 time period of our study. By contrast, unemployment also varies between countries but can also vary sharply within countries over time, as occurred during the global economic recession beginning in 2009 when unemployment spiked across Western democracies.

Our electoral institutions measure is (logged) average district magnitude, which denotes the degree to which representation is more majoritarian (lower district magnitude) or more proportional (higher district magnitude). We use the (logged) average district magnitude of the first tier, based on the data set compiled by Bormann and Golder (2013). The majoritarian systems in our study (the United States, UK, Canada, Australia, and France) all feature single-member district electoral systems and score at 0 on the (logged) district magnitude variable. The countries with the highest values (most proportional systems) include Germany, the Netherlands, and Norway, which all score slightly above 5. Most of the countries we analyze maintained the same electoral system across the time period of our study, so that virtually all the variation on this variable is between countries.

Table 4 reports descriptive statistics for our explanatory variables. For ease of interpretation we standardize our measures of elite polarization on all three dimensions (left–right, economics, and culture), so that a 0 value denotes that the measured intensity of elite polarization in the country-year scores at the average across the eighty-one elections in our study, while +1 denotes that elite polarization is one standard deviation above the average, and so on. The two right-most columns report the degree of between- and within-country variation of the variable values, which reflect whether the variations in each variable's values are primarily *between* countries or *within* countries at different time points. We see that elite policy polarization and unemployment levels vary substantially both *between* and *within* countries, which implies that we have the statistical leverage to parse out how temporal changes in these variables explain mass-level affective polarization within countries over time, in statistical analyses that control for country fixed effects. By contrast, income inequality varies substantially between countries but very little within countries over the time period of our study (1996–2017), while (logged) district magnitude varies between countries but is essentially static within countries. This lack of within-country variation implies that we cannot parse out the effects of income inequality and electoral systems on affective polarization based on within-countries analyses; instead we must rely on comparisons between countries.

Table 5 reports correlations between the values of the independent variables in our data set. Right–left elite ideological polarization correlates strongly with

**Table 4** Descriptive statistics of explanatory variables (N = 81)

| | Mean | Standard dDeviation | Minimum | Maximum | Between country variance | Within country variance |
|---|---|---|---|---|---|---|
| *Right–left elite polarization* | 0 | 1 | –1.78 | 2.69 | 0.79 | 0.66 |
| *Cultural elite polarization* | 0 | 1 | –1.48 | 4.08 | 0.77 | 0.66 |
| *Economic elite polarization* | 0 | 1 | –1.71 | 4.06 | 0.72 | 0.72 |
| *Gini (income inequality)* | 29.74 | 3.88 | 22.20 | 38.20 | 3.89 | 0.82 |
| *Unemployment* | 7.08 | 4.20 | 2.20 | 24.90 | 3.83 | 2.36 |
| *Electoral institutions (logged district magnitude)* | 2.40 | 1.92 | 0 | 6.01 | 1.86 | 0.08 |

*Notes.* Table 4 presents the descriptive statistics of our independent variables. The variables are defined in the body of the text.

**Table 5** Correlations between the independent variable levels

| | Cultural elite polarization | Economic elite polarization | Gini | Unem-ployment | Electoral institutions |
|---|---|---|---|---|---|
| Right–left elite polarization | 0.72*** | 0.69*** | –0.10 | 0.08 | –0.00 |
| Cultural elite polarization | – | 0.29*** | –0.13 | –0.15 | 0.15 |
| Economic elite polarization | – | – | –0.18* | 0.10 | –0.05 |
| Gini (income inequality) | – | – | – | 0.26** | –0.35*** |
| Unemployment | – | – | – | – | –0.13 |

* p < 0.1 ; ** p < 0.05 ; *** p < 0.01

*Notes.* Table 5 presents the correlations between our independent variables. The variables are defined in the body of the text.

elite economic and cultural polarization (at about r = 0.7), which is expected since the right–left measure includes both economic and cultural items from the Comparative Manifesto Project (CMP) data. The correlation between elite economic and cultural polarization is positive but weaker (r = 0.29, p < 0.01), denoting that parties that espouse more progressive, pro-welfare economic policies also tend to support more progressive positions on cultural issues. This weaker correlation suggests the value of analyzing the economic and cultural dimensions separately. Consistent with the findings of Lijphart (2010) and Iversen and Soskice (2015), income inequality correlates with less proportional voting systems (r = –0.35, p < 0.01). Unemployment correlates weakly with higher levels of income inequality (r = 0.26, p < 0.05), although as noted above the United States over the past twenty-five years is an exception, in that it has featured comparatively low unemployment but high income inequality. These correlations underscore the importance of estimating multivariate models that jointly control for these various predictive factors.

## 3.3 The Relationship between Affective Polarization and Our Explanatory Variables: Empirical Analyses

Figure 9 displays the bivariate relationships between affective polarization in mass publics (the vertical axis) and our three sets of explanatory variables: national economic conditions, political institutions, and elite ideological and policy polarization. Each dot in the figure represents a single case (country-election data point), and country abbreviations are located at the average value for each country.

We first discuss our elite polarization variables. We find no significant support for our expectation that elite ideological and policy polarization are associated with affective polarization when analyzing bivariate correlations: mass-level affective polarization appears only slightly higher, on average, in countries whose elites are more polarized on overall Left-Right ideology (Figure 9A) or on economic issues (Figure 9B) or cultural issues (Figure 9 C), and these relationships are not statistically significant.[24] Elite ideological and policy polarization thus fails to predict variation in affective polarization *between* countries. However, we show that intensifying elite cultural polarization within countries predicts affective polarization changes over time.

With respect to national economic conditions, affective polarization correlates strongly with both unemployment (r = 0.50, p < 0.01) and economic inequality

---

[24] Reiljan (2020) documents a stronger relationship between affective and elite-level ideological polarization. His study covers a larger number of countries as he does not limit his sample to Western democracies. Reiljan also uses a shorter time frame, drawing on waves 3 and 4 of the Comparative Study of Electoral Systems (covering the period 1996–2005) whereas we analyze data across the 1996–2017 period.

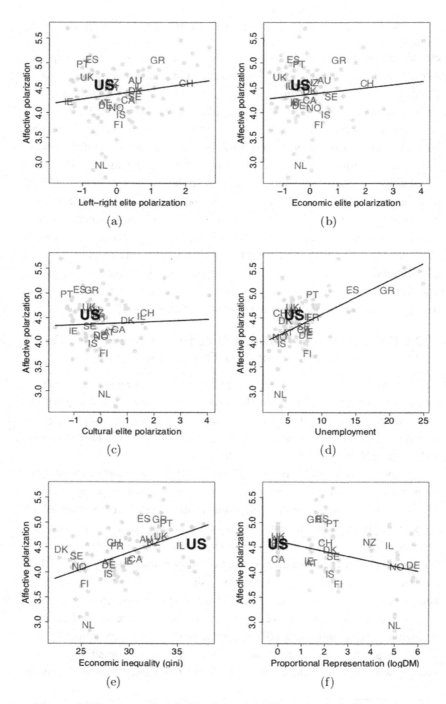

**Figure 9** Bi-variate relationships between affective polarization and our explanatory variables

**Note:** Figure 9 presents correlations between affective polarization and our explanatory variables. The explanatory variables on the x-axis are defined in the body of the text.

**Caption for Figure 9** (cont.)

Higher values on the y-axis denote higher levels of affective polarization in the mass public. Each dot represents a country-election observation. Country abbreviations display country averages.

(r = 0.47, p < 0.01), in cross-national comparisons. That is, mass-level affective polarization tends to be more intense in countries with higher levels of unemployment (Figure 9D) and with more pronounced income inequality (Figure 9E). These relationships provide preliminary support for our hypotheses that income inequality and unemployment intensify affective polarization in mass publics.

With respect to electoral institutions, specifically the proportionality of the electoral arena (Figure 9 F), we find initial support for our theoretical expectation: mass-level affective polarization tends to be higher in more majoritarian institutions (r = –0.34, p < 0.01), which supports Lijphart's claim that proportional systems give rise to gentler, more compromise-oriented politics. This supports to Drutman's (2019) claim that America's strict two-party system helps sustain intense affective polarization.

### 3.3.1 Multivariate Analyses

We next estimate the relationship between affective polarization (defined as the difference between in-party and out-party affective valuations) and the independent variables previously defined. First, we estimate a basic model to evaluate our hypotheses pertaining to elite ideological polarization (H1a), economic conditions (H2a, H2b), and electoral institutions (H3):

$$\text{Affective Polarization}_i(t) = b1 + b2[\text{elite left-right polarization}_i(t)]$$
$$+ b3[\text{income inequality}_i(t)] + b4[\text{unemployment}_i(t)]$$
$$+ b5[\text{logged District Magnitude}_i(t)] \quad (3)$$

where the subscript $i$ denotes the country in which the variable is being measured, and $t$ denotes the year of the CSES election survey. The elite ideological polarization hypothesis (H1a) implies that the coefficient on the [elite ideological polarization$_i(t)$] variable will be positive, denoting that elite ideological polarization intensifies affective polarization. The income inequality hypothesis (H2a) and the unemployment hypothesis (H2b) imply positive coefficients on the [income inequality$_i(t)$] and [unemployment$_i(t)$] variables, denoting that affective polarization is more intense where income inequality and unemployment are higher. Finally, the majoritarian institutions hypothesis (H3) implies that the coefficient on the [logged district magnitude$_i(t)$] variable will be negative, denoting that affective polarization is higher in countries that feature majoritarian electoral systems with low district magnitudes.

Next, we estimate a model that includes both economic and cultural elite ideological polarization, in order to evaluate our hypothesis that elite disagreements on cultural issues are more directly linked with affective polarization (H1b) than elite disagreements on economic issues:

$$\text{Affective Polarization}_i(t)] = b1 + b2[\text{elite economic polarization}_i(t)]$$
$$+ b3[\text{elite cultural Polarization}_i(t)]$$
$$+ b4[\text{income inequality}_i(t)] + b5[\text{unemployment}_i(t)]$$
$$+ b6[\text{logged District Magnitude}_i(t)] \qquad (4)$$

Our cultural primacy hypothesis implies a larger positive coefficient estimate on the [elite cultural polarization$_i(t)$] variable than on the [elite economic polarization$_i(t)$] variable, that is, that affective polarization in mass publics intensifies more in response to elite disputes over cultural issues than over economic issues. (Recall that the elite economic and cultural polarization variables are standardized, so that we can meaningfully compare their coefficients.) Our expectations for the other variables are the same as described.

We initially estimate the parameters of the models above (equations 3 and 4) without country fixed-effects. This is the best strategy for reliably estimating the relationship between affective polarization (our dependent variable) and levels of income inequality and (logged) district magnitude, because these independent variables display little to no variation within countries over the period of our study. In order to examine differences in affective polarization *within* countries over time, we estimate similar models with country fixed effects but without the income inequality and (logged) district magnitude variables, which are almost time invariant. These fixed effects models allow us to examine how over-time changes in unemployment and elite polarization on the left–right, economic, and cultural dimensions drive affective polarization changes within countries over time.

Table 6 reports parameter estimates for the left–right elite polarization models with and without country fixed effects (models 1 and 2 respectively), and the economics and cultural elite polarization models, again with and without country fixed effects (models 3 and 4). We estimate the models using ordinary least squares (OLS) with robust standard errors clustered by country. In all models, the dependent variable is our difference-based measure of mass-level affective polarization in the given country-year, for which higher values denote more intense polarization.

**Table 6** Analyses of affective polarization (N = 81)

| Independent vars | (1) | (2) | (3) | (4) |
|---|---|---|---|---|
| *Elite left-right polarization* | 0.099 (0.062) | 0.097 (0.064) | | |
| *Elite economic polarization* | | | 0.044 (0.046) | 0.003 (0.051) |
| *Elite cultural polarization* | | | 0.084 (0.062) | 0.170*** (0.062) |
| *Income inequality* | 0.046** (0.018) | | 0.047** (0.020) | |
| *Unemployment level* | 0.052*** (0.014) | 0.052*** (0.014) | 0.055*** (0.013) | 0.054*** (0.015) |
| *Logged* District Magnitude | −0.052 (0.037) | | −0.056 (0.041) | |
| *Intercept* | 2.752*** (0.569) | 4.300*** (0.071) | 2.716*** (0.623) | 4.387*** (0.082) |
| *Country fixed effects* | No | Yes | No | Yes |
| Adjusted $R^2$ | 0.405 | 0.758 | 0.439 | 0.704 |

$* p < 0.1$ ; $** p < 0.05$ ; $*** p < 0.01$

*Notes.* The dependent variable in these analyses is [*affective polarization$_i$(t)*], defined as the observed intensity of mass-level affective polarization in country *i* in *year t*. The independent variables are defined in the text. The top number in each cell is the unstandardized coefficient, the number in parentheses below is the standard error. The OLS regression models were estimated with standard errors clustered on countries.

The results reported in Table 6 support several conclusions. First, once we control for economic conditions and electoral institutions, our estimate on the [elite left–right polarization$_i$(t)] variable is statistically insignificant in all of our models (i.e., there is no detectable relationship between elite ideological polarization and affective polarization). Thus, we *do not* find support for our elite ideological polarization hypothesis (H1a), that Ideological polarization between rival parties' elites intensifies mass-level affective polarization.

As we noted earlier, the left–right (liberal–conservative) dimension is a "super-dimension" that encompasses both economic debates over income redistribution and state intervention in the economy, and cultural debates over national identity and moral values. This distinction holds for both Western Europe (e.g., Hooghe and Marks 2018; Kitschelt 1994) and the United States (Carmines and D'Amico 2015; Ellis and Stimson 2012; Lupton et al. 2015). Our cultural primacy hypothesis (H1b) posits that affective polarization in mass publics intensifies more in response to elite disputes over cultural issues than over economic issues. In our model without country fixed effects (model 3), we find no significant evidence that elite polarization on either economic or cultural issues predicts more intense affective polarization; that is, the coefficient estimates on the [elite economic polarization$_i(t)$] and [elite cultural polarization$_i(t)$] variables are insignificant. However, when we incorporate country fixed effects (model 4), we estimate that elite polarization *on cultural issues, but not on economic issues*, drives affective polarization. That is, we estimate that, over time, within-country increases in elite cultural polarization are associated with intensifying mass-level affective polarization. The coefficient on our [elite cultural polarization$_i(t)$] variable in model 4, +0.170 ($p < 0.01$), implies that a 1 standard deviation increase in elite cultural polarization predicts an 0.17-point increase on our affective polarization variable[25] – about a third of the standard variation of this variable. As suggested by Sides et al. (2018), cultural divides feel "angrier" than divides over economic policy.

As discussed previously, we place more weight on the relationships we estimate in models that control for country fixed effects (i.e., relationships based on over time changes *within countries* rather than differences *between countries*) because between-country differences may be driven by factors we cannot account for in our analyses including countries' democratic histories, their media regimes, regional and linguistic cleavages, and so on. Hence we see our estimates for the economics and politics model with country fixed effects (model 4) as providing important support for our cultural primacy hypothesis (H1b).

With respect to this discussion, we emphasize that our lack of statistically significant findings on elite economic polarization *do not* prove that elite economic disputes are unrelated to mass-level affective polarization: absence of a statistically significant relationship does not prove that no such relationship exists. As discussed, there are theoretical reasons to expect elite economic disputes to intensify mass-level affective polarization – although we have argued that these economic effects should be weaker than the effects of elite cultural disputes. And, our findings might change if it were feasible to extend our analyses over a longer time span than the 1996–2017 period of our study. Thus our non-finding on the relationship between elite economic disputes and mass-level polarization prompts us to label this relationship as "unproven," not "non-existent." That being said, our estimates *do* support our theoretical arguments that elite cultural disputes intensify mass-level affective polarization more strongly than economic disputes. On this basis we proceed.

---

[25] Recall that our elite polarization variable values are standardized, so that our coefficient estimates on these variables denote the predicted effect of a one standard deviation change.

We also find strong support for our hypotheses on the effects of national economic conditions. First, we estimate that affective polarization is more intense in countries with higher economic inequality (H2a), in analyses that control for elite ideological polarization (model 1), and when controlling for elite economic and cultural polarization (model 3). These estimates support our income inequality hypothesis, that higher levels of income inequality intensify mass-level affective polarization (H2a). Our estimates on the [income inequality$_i(t)$] variable are nearly identical in both models (+0.046 for model 1, +0.047 in model 3, $p < 0.05$), and imply that a one standard deviation change in the level of income inequality (i.e., 3.88 units on the gini inequality coefficient) is associated with a roughly 0.18-unit increase in the predicted intensity of mass-level affective polarization – almost the same as the predicted effect of a one standard deviation change in elite cultural polarization. These estimates for multivariate models are consistent with the bivariate relationship between inequality and affective polarization displayed in Figure 9. Note, however, that these estimates are for models that do not control for country fixed effects: as noted, economic inequality tends to change very slowly over time within Western democracies, and since our data cover a relatively short time span (1996–2017) nearly all of the variation on the income inequality variable is *between* countries rather than *within* countries over time (see Table 4). Thus we cannot reliably estimate the effects of within-country inequality changes on affective polarization, and the between-country analyses we report do not control for differences between countries' democratic histories, their media regimes, and so on. We therefore interpret the cross-national relationship between income inequality and affective polarization with caution: while it supports our hypothesis that inequality intensifies affective polarization (H2a), we acknowledge the possibility of unmeasured variable bias. Moreover, it is possible that affective polarization also drives inequality, not vice versa: for instance, inequality may create the type of policy gridlock that results in polarization and policy drift (Pierson and Schickler 2020).

Second, we estimate that affective polarization is significantly more intense in countries and in time periods with higher unemployment – estimates that support our unemployment hypothesis (H2b) that unemployment intensifies mass-level affective polarization. Importantly, this relationship holds across all of our models, including those both with and without country fixed effects. This implies that affective polarization in the mass public tends to be more intense in countries with higher unemployment rates, but also that, over time, affective polarization tends to intensify *within* countries when unemployment increases. Both relationships are important since some countries in our data set display consistently higher unemployment than others, but unemployment also varies substantially within countries over time: in particular, most of the countries in our study displayed sharp unemployment spikes during the global economic recession beginning in 2008–9. The coefficient estimates on the [unemployment$_i(t)$] variable are consistent across all of our models, ranging from +0.052 to +0.055 ($p < 0.01$ in every model), and imply that a one standard deviation change in the unemployment rate (i.e., 4.2 percentage points) is associated with a roughly 0.22-unit increase in the predicted intensity of mass-level affective polarization. And because this relationship is robust to controls for country fixed effects, we believe our estimates provide strong evidence in support of our unemployment hypothesis (H2b).

While unemployment (and political economic factors more broadly) has not been widely studied in affective polarization research in either the United States (e.g., Klein 2020) or abroad (e.g., Reiljan 2020), our estimates suggest that it significantly influences partisan animosity. In order to substantiate this conclusion we reestimated our models while omitting Greece, Spain, and Portugal, the countries that suffered the most extreme levels of unemployment during the period of our study. These analyses, which we report in Appendix 3.3 online, continued to identify a significant relationship between unemployment and affective polarization.

Finally, we turn to effects of electoral institutions (H3). When looking at bivariate relationships, we found a correlation between greater proportionality and lower affective polarization (see Figure 9F). However, the results reported in Table 6 suggest that this relationship is statistically insignificant, once we control for elite policy disagreements and economic conditions. These estimates *do not* support the majoritarian institutions hypothesis (H3), that affective polarization is more intense in countries with more majoritarian political institutions.

*Electoral institutions' independent effects on in-party liking and out-party dislike.* Surprised by the lack of empirical support for H3, we separately analyzed how electoral institutions are related to the two components of affective polarization, in-party liking and out-party dislike. These bivariate relationships are displayed in Figure 10A (for out-party dislike) and Figure 10B (for in-party liking). Recall that higher values of out-party dislike denote more *negative* out-party affective evaluations, and higher values of in-party liking denote more *positive* affective out-party affective evaluations. We see that more majoritarian electoral systems, operationalized as lower (average) district magnitude, are characterized by both more negative out-party feelings (Figure 10A) *and* more negative in-party affective evaluations (Figure 10B). These bivariate relationships already point at the warmer affective climate of more proportional systems, raising the possibility that what Lijphart (2010) characterizes as the "kinder, gentler" climate of more proportional, consensual

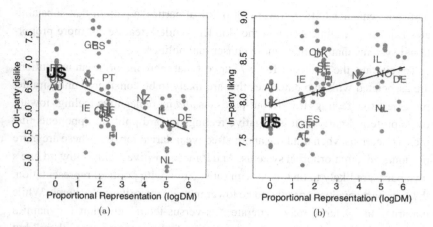

**Figure 10** Bi-variate relationships between electoral system and partisan affective evaluations

**Note:** Figure 10 displays correlations between in-party and out-party affective evaluations and electoral proportionality. Our measure of electoral proportionality is logged average district magnitude. Higher values on the y-axis denote more intense out-party dislike (subfigure a) and warmer in-party liking (subfigure b). Each dot represents a country-election observation. Country abbreviations show country averages.

institutions manifests itself in warmer feelings toward both in-parties *and* out-parties.

To further probe this issue, we estimate the parameters of regression models similar to those reported in Table 6, but this time taking as our dependent variables the two components of affective polarization: out-party dislike and in-party liking. Table 7 reports the results, which substantiate that electoral institutions matter when analyzing out-party and in-party affective evaluations separately.[26] As electoral systems become more proportional, partisans express less negative affective evaluations of out-parties as well as more positive affective evaluations of their own party. That is, more proportional electoral systems are associated with partisans' improved affect toward *all* parties, both their own and its opponents. Since our overall affective polarization measure is defined as the *difference* between in-party liking and out-party liking, these dynamics cancel each other out to some degree – which is why we find no statistically significant relationship between difference-based affective polarization and electoral institutions in Table 6. This however should not lead us to overlook the strong relationship between electoral system proportionality and

---

[26] In the models reported in Table 7, we account for elite ideological polarization on the overall left–right dimension. The results remain substantively similar if we control instead for elite polarization on economic and cultural issues.

partisans' enhanced affect toward all political parties, a pattern that substantiates Lijphart's arguments about the "kinder, gentler" features of more proportional systems that facilitate more consensual politics.

To reiterate, the results in Table 7 suggest that more majoritarian institutions are associated with two outcomes that are likely to be considered undesirable: more negative feelings toward out-partisans *and* more negative feelings toward one's preferred party. If it is negative feelings toward political opponents that most concern us when thinking about affective polarization, then these are more pronounced in majoritarian systems. And if more positive feelings toward one's own party are likely to be linked with satisfaction with political representation, these in-party evaluations tend to be lower in more majoritarian systems. While majoritarian systems may generate "us-versus-them" emotional dynamics (Drutman 2019), this is reflected in negative feelings toward the "them" but not in more positive feelings toward the "us" – indeed majoritarian systems, including the United States, tend to feature partisans who display comparatively little enthusiasm for their own party.

Readers familiar with Lijphart's research may note that electoral institutions are only one feature of his conceptualization of "kinder, gentler" political systems. While we think electoral systems are particularly important as they

**Table 7** Analyses of in-party and out-party affective evaluations

| Independent vars | Out-party dislike | In-party liking |
|---|---|---|
| *Elite left–right ideological polarization* | 0.005 | 0.081 |
|  | (0.055) | (0.056) |
| *Income inequality* | 0.042*** | −0.004 |
|  | (0.015) | (0.015) |
| *Unemployment level* | 0.076*** | −0.021** |
|  | (0.009) | (0.010) |
| *Logged (District Magnitude)* | −0.133*** | 0.072** |
|  | (0.030) | (0.027) |
| *Intercept* | 4.803*** | 8.211*** |
|  | (0.503) | (0.473) |
| *N* | 81 | 81 |
| Adjusted $R^2$ | 0.636 | 0.217 |

* $p < 0.1$ ; ** $p < 0.05$ ; *** $p < 0.01$

*Notes.* The independent variables are defined in the text. The top number in each cell is the unstandardized coefficient, the number in parentheses below is the standard error. The OLS regression models were estimated with standard errors clustered on countries.

shape the rules of partisan competition, we estimated additional models using Lijphart's "executive dimensions" – an overall measure of the extent to which a country's political institutions incentivize power sharing. This measure includes additional factors besides electoral systems, namely federalism, executive–legislative relations, and interest group pluralism. As we report in Appendix 3.4, our substantive conclusions remain the same: consensual institutions that incentivize power-sharing are associated with more positive in-party *and* out-party evaluations.

While we cannot provide direct evidence for the mechanism at work within this framework of country-level analyses, we suspect that cooperation in coalition governments plays a major role in diffusing out-party negative sentiments. There is evidence that people perceive parties that govern together to be more ideologically similar to one another than is implied by these parties stated positions (Fortunato and Stevenson 2013). If people rely on coalition heuristics when forming affective evaluations of out-parties, they may adopt more positive feelings toward coalition partners, when controlling for objective party position measures (Gidron et al. 2019b). As the comparative affective polarization literature develops, we expect future research to shed more light on this point.

There are several additional insights that emerge from Table 7. Economic inequality is predictive of greater out-party dislike, all else equal, but it is not a statistically significant predictor of in-party affective evaluations. Higher unemployment is correlated with more negative affective evaluations toward both in-parties and toward out-parties. These findings emphasize the need to consider the drivers of in-party and out-party feelings independently (Bankert 2020).

## 3.4 Discussion: Situating American Affective Polarization in Comparative Perspective

Our statistical analyses uncovered that partisan affective evaluations are associated with three factors: elite polarization on cultural issues; adverse national economic conditions, namely economic inequality and unemployment; and electoral institutions. In this last section, we situate the American case within our broader sample of Western democracies.

### 3.4.1 American Ideological Polarization: The Rise of Elite Cultural Polarization

Our results show that affective polarization intensifies within countries in tandem with elite disagreements on cultural issues, more so than on economic issues. That is, the politics of "who we are" appears more emotionally polarizing than the politics of "who gets what." The observation that issues of national identity "feel angrier" than do questions of redistribution and the welfare state (Sides et al. 2018) is supported by our cross-national analyses of changes in affective polarization within countries. These findings suggest that the growing elite polarization on cultural issues in the United States stands may be a major driver of American affective polarization. Within the time period covered in our data, the United States has experienced a steep increase in elite cultural polarization, compared to other Western democracies. In 1996, the first US data point in our study, the United States was *the least* polarized country in terms of cultural issues: 1.7 standard deviation below the mean of the cultural elite polarization average levels. By 2016, it had become one of the most culturally polarized countries in our sample, a bit more than one standard deviation above the mean. That is, cultural elite ideological polarization in the United States has *increased by more than two and a half standard deviations*. This is a sharper increase than the rise in elite economic polarization that the United States experienced within the same time. Indeed, our manifesto-based measure implies that elite cultural polarization intensified more sharply in the United States than in any other country in our study.[27]

The growing American elite cultural polarization that we document resonates with other sources on recent transformations in American politics. For instance, Goren and Chapp (2017, 124) refer to the most recent time period as a moment of intense "cultural polarization" in American politics. The divergence between the two American parties on issues of race of course goes back farther in time, with the 1960s featuring prominently as a watershed moment on cultural issues and racial questions in particular (Schickler 2016). This does not necessarily imply that America is more divided on racial issues today than during the civil rights era, but instead that political parties have sorted on and politicized these divisions in ways that had not occurred in prior eras. Cultural polarization has intensified since the 1990s, especially during the Obama presidency and the rise of the Tea Party movement within the Republican Party (Skocpol and Williamson 2011; Tesler 2016). This process of elite cultural polarization has reached its current apex following the election of President Donald Trump and the emphasis of his campaign on issues of national identity (Bonikowski et al. 2019; Sides et al. 2018).

---

[27] While the United States increased by 2.8 standard deviations on the elite cultural polarization measure across the period of our study, no other Western party system in our study saw an increase of more than 2 standard deviations.

We note that our findings on the primacy of elite cultural disputes stand in contrast to previous important work, which linked American affective polarization more strongly to economic rather than cultural issues (Iyengar et al. (2012, 422). Abramowitz and Webster (2017, 632) note that

> Specifically, conservative views on social welfare policy were strongly associated with negative feelings toward Barack Obama and the Democratic Party and with positive feelings toward Mitt Romney and the Republican Party. Likewise, conservative views on abortion policy and gay rights were associated with negative feelings toward Obama and the Democratic Party and with positive feelings toward Romney and the Republican Party, although these relationships were considerably weaker than those for social welfare policy.

One reason for the discrepancy between our findings and those of Abramowitz and Webster (2017) is that these authors analyze individual-level affect, while the unit of analysis in our study is the country-election level. On a more theoretical level, these contrasting finding call for further attention to the porous boundaries between economic and cultural issues. Welfare issues such as "government aid to Blacks" (Abramowitz and Webster 2017, 628), are plausibly infused with strong cultural overtones (Tesler 2016; Gilens 1999). That is, some economic attitudes – such as welfare benefits for racial and ethnic minorities – may be linked with cultural worldviews in ways that blur the distinction between these two dimensions.

### 3.4.2 American Economics: The Contrasting Implications of High Inequality and Low Unemployment

How do American economic conditions compare to those of other Western countries? The United States has the highest average level of economic inequality in our sample, with an average Gini score of around 37: higher than other Anglo-American democracies such as the United Kingdom (33) and Canada (31), and far above more egalitarian Western European countries such as Sweden (24) and Denmark (23). Of course, this comes as no surprise: the high levels of American economic inequality over the last few decades are thoroughly documented (Hager 2018; Saez 2012).

As we discussed earlier, economic inequality is a slow-moving variable, one that is almost time-invariant within countries over the 1996–2017 time period we cover. We therefore cannot reliably estimate the impact, within countries, of over-time changes in Gini on affective polarization changes. Our findings reflect correlations across countries: where inequality is higher, affective polarization is more intense. Previous work has documented a strong relationship between economic inequality and elite-level ideological polarization in the American Congress (McCarty et al. 2006) and affective polarization across the American states (Stewart et al. 2020). We expand this US-focused research with the cross-national finding that higher economic inequality predicts more intense mass-level affective polarization, across Western publics.

At the same time, the historically low American unemployment levels during the 2010s likely helped prevent affective polarization from rising even higher. Unemployment increased in the United States during the Great Recession, and had reached 8.1 percent in 2012 only to decline to 4.9 percent in 2016. Without overlooking the devastating consequences of the Great Recession to many Americans' livelihoods, these unemployment numbers were far lower than those suffered in many other Western democracies, most starkly in Southern Europe. In Greece, for instance, unemployment spiked following the economic crisis, from around 10 percent in the 2009 election to 24 percent in the 2012 election and 25 percent in the elections of 2015. Portugal's unemployment rate also increased by more than 10 percentage points in the aftermath of the Eurocrisis. And indeed, both countries have seen major increases in affective polarization during this time period. The severe economic downturn has led to growing ideological polarization in Southern Europe, and in Greece to a complete transformation of the party system following the rise of radical parties (Altiparmakis 2019; da Silva and Mendes 2019). Our analyses add to existing accounts of these transformations, by documenting that higher unemployment may have also intensified mass-level affective polarization.

### 3.4.3 American Majoritarian Institutions and Partisan Affective Evaluations

Our findings regarding electoral institutions and affective polarization call for some nuance. While we did not uncover a strong statistical relationship between electoral rules and affective polarization, our difference-based affective polarization measure serves to mask the impact of electoral rules on partisan affect. We find that more majoritarian institutions predict greater dislike toward partisan opponents *and* cooler feelings toward one's own party – that is, majoritarian institutions depress partisans' affect toward parties in general. This suggests that more proportional electoral systems are related to two potentially desirable outcomes: less dislike of opposing parties and warmer feelings toward one's own in party. This finding supports the recent emphasis on electoral institutions as a major root driver of partisan resentment in the United States (Drutman 2019; Kuo 2014).

The United States is an outlier among Western democracies, with its strict two-party system. Our coding of electoral rules is based on the district magnitude, which equals 1 in the United States – as well as in Australia, Canada, France and the United Kingdom. Yet all these countries other than the United States feature more than two viable parties. France and Canada have developed multiparty systems for reasons that are beyond the scope of our discussion. Even in the United Kingdom, the Conservatives and Labour retained their dominance, yet other parties – such as the Scottish National Party – have received substantial electoral support at certain moments, and the Liberal Democrats gained enough power to serve as coalition partners between 2010–15. It is only in the United States that we find complete two-party dominance. In this respect, our measure of electoral institutions may be a conservative one since it does not capture differences in party system configuration between different countries with a district magnitude of 1.

## 3.5 Conclusions

In this section, we have applied our comparative strategy to analyze the ideological, economic, and institutional correlates of affective polarization across twenty Western democracies between 1996 and 2016. In analyses that focus on variations within countries over time, we found evidence that growing elite disputes on cultural issues drive affective polarization, while we did not detect evidence of a comparable effect of elite economic disagreements. In comparisons both between countries and within countries over time, we showed that higher unemployment is strongly associated with intense affective polarization, while in comparisons across countries we documented higher affective polarization in countries with higher economic inequality. Finally, we documented more intense out-party dislike – and more tepid in-party liking – in countries with more majoritarian institutions.

Our findings suggest that the relationship between elite ideological disagreements and affective polarization deserve a second look. While the majority of research on the relationship between affective polarization and elite ideological polarization focuses on elite disagreements on the overall left–right (i.e., liberal–conservative) dimension (e.g., Rogowski and Sutherland 2015; Lelkes 2019), our findings emphasize the need to distinguish between the effects of elite disagreements on economics versus culture. And in contrast to research that connected American affective polarization to economic elite disagreements, our cross-national perspective identified stronger effects of elite cultural disputes. As we have noted, one way to square the tension between our results and previous research is by considering the potential cultural and racial interpretations of some economic issues (such as welfare) in American politics.

Our analyses also point toward the value of integrating research on affective polarization and political economy. Our findings that unemployment and (in cross-national comparisons) income inequality strongly predict affective polarization are relevant for political developments in the aftermath of the Great Recession. The post-recession decline in unemployment implies less intense affective polarization as Western democracies recovered from the financial crisis. Yet if the economic recovery is uneven (Saez 2012), then the long-term negative effects of growing income inequality may counteract the beneficial short-term effects of employment gains.

As we finish writing this Element in August 2020, we confronted the prospect of a severe and possibly long-term economic downturn following the outbreak of the coronavirus, in the United States and across Western democracies. Our empirical analyses suggest that if Western publics suffer prolonged unemployment increases, this may intensify affective polarization. In a more positive scenario, however, standing united against a common health threat could activate a shared sense of national identity, which may temper affective polarization (Levendusky 2018) – although we see little evidence of diminishing partisan disputes in the United States to this point. In years to come, the readers of this Element will be in better position than we are now to judge the push and pull of these contrasting effects. For now, our findings suggest that the unifying effects of fighting a health crisis may be necessary to counteract the divisive, affectively polarizing effects of rising unemployment.

Our analyses raise causal inference questions, especially with respect to our findings regarding income inequality and electoral institutions. While we document strong correlations between affective evaluations, income inequality, and majoritarian institutions in comparisons *between* countries, we cannot reliably estimate these relationships via comparisons *within* countries over time: institutions, and to a lesser degree economic inequality, are too sticky. These cross-national comparisons may be problematic, because the countries in our study differ in ways we cannot measure (or only measure imperfectly): a partial list includes differences in partisan media, in economic regimes, and in countries' democratic histories that influence current patterns of mass partisanship. Yet if we discount cross-national comparisons, it may be impossible to estimate how income inequality and institutions influence affective polarization; there is simply too little within-country variation on these variables. This is a subject for future research.

## 4 Conclusions

Americans increasingly distrust and dislike partisan opponents; that is, they are increasingly *affectively polarized*. A Pew Research report from 2019 noted that the 2016 election was "unfolding against a backdrop of intense partisan division and animosity," and since then, "the level of division and animosity, including negative sentiments among partisans toward the members of the opposing party, has only deepened." While meaningful *policy* polarization may help citizens understand parties' programmatic differences and stabilize party systems (Levendusky 2010; Lupu 2015), intense *affective* polarization depresses trust and cooperation across party lines (McConnell et al. 2018) and can undermine democratic norms and institutions (Hetherington and Rudolph 2015; Levitsky and Ziblatt 2018; McCoy and Somer 2019). As we write this in August 2020, at the outset of what promises to be a vitriolic and divisive general election campaign, America's partisan affective divisions appear deeper than ever.

We have studied American affective polarization through a comparative lens, by analyzing cross-national and over-time trends across eighty-one elections in twenty Western publics (including the United States) between 1996 and 2017, using survey data from the Comparative Study of Electoral Systems (CSES) which includes common items measuring citizens' partisanship and their party thermometer ratings (i.e., how much they like and dislike each major party in their country). Following the standard approach in the American politics literature, we defined affective polarization as the difference between partisan survey respondents' thermometer ratings of their in-party (the party to which they are attached) and their ratings of out-parties (i.e., their preferred party's opponents). We have addressed several questions of pressing interest to American political observers, including: Is the US public more affectively polarized than other Western publics? Is America's intensifying affective polarization unusual, or is this part of a general increase across Western democracies? And: What can the cross-national and temporal patterns we identify tell us about the possible economic, institutional, and policy-based drivers of affective polarization, in the United States and across Western publics?

## 4.1 Summarizing Our Key Findings

Our first key finding is that while American affective polarization has intensified in recent decades, it is *not* an outlier among Western publics.

Across the 1996–2017 time period of our study, the US public has shifted from being somewhat *less* affectively polarized than most Western publics in the mid 1990s to *more* intensely polarized by the elections of 2012 and 2016 – yet even in 2012–16 American affective polarization was not exceptionally intense compared to many other Western polities including Britain, Australia, New Zealand, and (especially) Spain, Greece, and Portugal. On the other hand, dislike of partisan opponents is intensifying more rapidly in the United States than in most other Western publics. In short, to the extent we consider affective polarization as a "public bad," America's political environment has deteriorated over the past twenty-plus years; this is *not* part of a general trend across Western publics; and, America's affective polarization level in 2012–16 was somewhat intense – although not an outlier – compared to other Western publics.

Our conclusion that American affective polarization is "only" above average – but not exceptionally intense – in comparative perspective may cheer readers who are dismayed by the intense inter-party hostility they observe in contemporary American politics. Be this as it may, we are deeply troubled by the pernicious political, societal, and economic consequences of American affective polarization that scholars have documented. And from a comparative perspective, there is room for concern about the costs of partisan division and animosity in other Western polities, some of which has transpired after the endpoint of our study (which stops in 2017, the most recent year for which CSES survey data is currently available). Recent events such as the rise of far-right parties across many Western European countries, the bitter divisions associated with Britain's withdrawal from the European Union (Brexit), and the fragmentation of many Western party systems may prompt Americanists to question whether our finding that American affective polarization is "only" above average in comparative perspective is cause for comfort.

Beyond documenting cross-national and over-time affective polarization trends, we have analyzed three country-level factors that may illuminate variations in affective polarization, both between countries and within countries over time: elite polarization on economic and cultural issues, national economic conditions pertaining to unemployment and income inequality, and electoral institutions. We showed that affective polarization intensifies within countries during periods when party elites clash more sharply over cultural debates about "who we are" (such as debates over multiculturalism and national identity), while we detect no comparable relationship between affective polarization and elite economic disputes over "who gets what." This pattern is important for American politics, since the United States displays the sharpest increase in elite cultural polarization across Western democracies over the period of our study, based on content analyses of parties' election manifestos (platforms). Our analyses suggest that one reason American partisans increasingly distrust and dislike out-parties is precisely because of this elite cultural polarization – and, we believe that America's "culture wars" have further intensified in the years since 2016, the last US data point in our study. While scholars have extensively studied how the rise of cultural issues reshapes voting behavior and electoral strategies (Abou-Chadi and Wagner 2019; Hillygus and Shields 2008; Hooghe and Marks 2018; Kitschelt 1994; Kriesi et al. 2008), we find that elite cultural disputes also intensify mass-level affective polarization.

We emphasize that the politicization of some cultural issues, notably LGBT + rights and race relations, can be viewed positively since the alternative has often been a compromise that suppressed disadvantaged social groups (Klein 2020). From this perspective, affective polarization may be the price of social progress.

Our findings on the relationship between national economic conditions and affective polarization should encourage a dialogue between affective polarization researchers, who often emphasize psychological individual-level mechanisms, and political economists, who highlight structural factors. The cross-national correlation we uncover between income inequality and more intense affective polarization resonates with previous work that identifies growing economic inequities as a source of partisan resentment in the United States (Levitsky and Ziblatt 2018; Stewart et al. 2020). However, this study requires a longer time horizon than the 1996–2017 period of our study, since income inequality levels change very slowly over time across Western democracies.

Our finding that unemployment drives affective polarization is relevant for political developments in the aftermath of the Great Recession, and possibly for politics during and after the COVID-19 pandemic. American unemployment levels during the late 2010s dropped to a nearly fifty-year low – yet affective polarization in the United States reached a postwar high. If American unemployment levels revert toward their historic norms, let alone levels associated with a deep recession due to the coronavirus crisis, this may further inflame inter-party hostility between Democrats and Republicans. The same warning applies to other Western democracies that suffer long-term economic damage from this pandemic. That being said, economic downturns during and after the coronavirus outbreak may differ from other postwar economic recessions, which could be more directly linked to economic policies such as deregulation (from the perspective of voters and politicians on the left) or irresponsible spending (from the perspective of those on the right). Fighting the spread of the coronavirus may also generate a rally-round-the-flag effect that primes people to prioritize their national – not their partisan – identity, which has been shown to defuse affective polarization (Levendusky 2018). The implications of this historic moment may hinge on the narratives and interpretive frames that Americans – along with citizens in other Western democracies – rely on to make sense of what may be, as we complete this Element, a historic economic downturn. While we hope for the best, the deep partisan divisions we currently observe in Americans' response to the pandemic, over issues such as the value of wearing face masks and social distancing – or even over whether we confront a genuine health crisis as opposed to a "media hoax" – tempers our optimism that the pandemic will prompt Americans to bridge their partisan divide.

Finally, we have documented a relationship between electoral institutions and partisan affective evaluations. More majoritarian electoral systems, notably the single-member district, are associated with partisans' more negative feelings toward opposing parties *and* with less positive feelings toward their own party. On the one hand, these relationships do not necessarily imply that single-member districts intensify overall affective polarization levels, since cooler feelings toward one's in-party *defuse* difference-based affective polarization, while greater hostility toward out-parties *intensifies* it. On the other hand, to the extent we are most concerned with partisans' scorn and hostility toward opponents, our findings substantiate Lijphart's (2010) classic arguments on the merits of the "kinder, gentler" politics fostered by proportional, consensual institutions, and these findings align with policy proposals for electoral reforms in the United States as a means to defuse partisan animosity. Our conclusions here rely on cross-national comparisons, since Western democracies rarely overhaul their electoral institutions. Future research should probe the mechanism at work behind this correlation between electoral laws and partisan affect.

While proportional systems are associated with positive partisan affect, they should not be seen as a panacea to defuse affective polarization. Proportional systems provide more electoral opportunities for populist, radical parties to enter parliament (Norris 2005; Norris and Inglehart 2019). These populist radical parties, especially on the right, are in turn strongly disliked by mainstream parties' supporters (Helbling and Jungkunz 2020; Kaltwasser and Mudde 2018; Reiljan 2020). However, we note that while populist parties can more easily achieve representation in proportional, multiparty systems, they practically never rule alone in these coalition-oriented countries. In two-party systems, by contrast, there is the danger that populist factions and candidates may take control over one of the governing parties (Drutman 2019, pp. 228–229). Thus winner-take-all systems are not immune to populism and may paradoxically make it easier for populists to control the executive branch.

## 4.2 Exploring the Structural Underpinnings of Affective Polarization in the United States and Abroad

Shifting the focus away from universal psychological motivations to contextual, country-level factors, our work adopts a different starting point that highlights the structural underpinning – in terms of ideology, political economy, and electoral institutions – of partisan animosity. That being said, we see the psychological and structural perspectives as complementary, and we hope future work integrates them. Our study of the structural correlates of affective polarization also highlights the potentials and limitations of proposed remedies for partisan resentment. Some work emphasizes how adopting a more civil, collegial tone toward political opponents in public discourse may temper affective polarization (Druckman et al. 2019). Our findings suggest, however, that affective polarization is also rooted in deeper economic and political structures, which require concerted political efforts to reform. While we endorse civility between competing political elites, our results suggest that defusing political animosity also requires addressing structural features within Western democracies.

There are additional structural, country-level factors we have not considered here, which suggest directions for future research. These include the structure of national and local media markets and access to broadband internet, which shape citizens' exposure to political information that may affect partisan affective evaluations (Benkler et al. 2018; Lelkes et al. 2017; Tsfati and Nir 2017). Especially in light of the growing number of protests that has swept the United States during 2020, one might also integrate research on social movements and mass protests (Bremer et al. 2020), which occur outside the electoral arena yet may generate emotional responses that color political evaluations. We might also explore how affective polarization is related to the characteristics of mass publics such as political interest (Ward and Tavits 2019), and to political elites' attributes including their gender, race, and religion. Finally, we suspect that media reports that reflect on political elites' competence, integrity and leadership ability – what Stokes (1963) labelled "valence issues" – influence citizens' party evaluations, and through this affective polarization (Clark 2009). Such cross-national comparisons may illuminate affective polarization in the United States and across Western publics.

## 4.3 The Comparative Study of American Polarization: Challenges and Future Steps

The United States represents the most widely studied case of mass- and elite-level polarization – yet it is not the only case. We hope we have convinced readers that a comparative perspective can illuminate affective polarization patterns in the United States and across Western democracies, in at least two ways. First, these comparisons provide a benchmark for assessing the intensity and trajectory of American affective polarization. Second, the comparative patterns we identify illuminate important correlates of affective polarization including electoral institutions, economic conditions and elite policy disputes, which are difficult to detect when examining the American case in isolation.

Reflecting on promising directions for the American and comparative polarization literatures, we see merit in more descriptive work that situates American polarization – affective polarization, but also ideological polarization and partisan sorting – within a comparative framework. This approach could address basic questions such as: Does the US public hold more or less extreme policy views than citizens in other Western publics? And: Has the ideological sorting of the American electorate – the process whereby conservatives have gravitated toward the Republican Party and liberals toward the Democratic Party – made the US party system more distinct from or more similar to other Western party systems? Before we can explain these variations, we must first document them. The comparative polarization literature, which takes the American case as its starting point, is at a stage where "more description" is in order (Gerring 2012).

One challenge to the comparative study of American affective polarization is the lack of cross-nationally and temporally comparable measures of citizens' feelings, perceptions, and behaviors across party lines. In this Element, we have analyzed the thermometer feelings survey question, which asks respondents to rate how much they like or dislike parties in their country. As discussed in Section 2, this is the only available survey-based measure of cross-party feelings across a large number of countries and across time. It is important to analyze and compare other measures such as feelings toward partisans (rather than parties), citizens' preferences for social distance (such as partisans' attitudes toward out-partisans as family members), and stereotypes toward opposing partisans (Druckman and Levendusky 2019). There is also a need for cross-nationally comparable behavioral measures that capture discrimination across party lines (Carlin and Love 2018; Sheffer 2020). Collecting these data will allow scholars to provide more nuanced insights, when situating American affective polarization in comparative perspective.

We also confront measurement challenges. To facilitate cross-national and over-time comparisons of American affective polarization, we have opted to measure affective polarization at the country-year level. This allowed us to compare, for instance, the United States in 1996 versus 2016, as well as the United States in 2016 versus Greece in 2015. Yet one can also analyze affective polarization at lower levels than the country-year. For instance, in the multiparty systems found in most Western democracies outside the United States, one can analyze affective polarization between different *pairs* of parties, in order to answer the question "Who dislikes whom?" (Gidron et al. 2019b). One can also analyze affective polarization at the individual level, in order to understand whether cross-party hostility and distrust is related to individual characteristics such as political interest, income, age, gender, partisanship, and ideology (Wagner 2020).

With respect to partisanship and ideology, there is evidence for asymmetries across the American partisan divide in media consumption: as Benkler et al. (2018, 23) note when discussing the 2016 US elections, it is "the insularity of right-wing media and audiences from the corrective function of professional journalism that made that segment of the overall media ecosystem more susceptible to political clickbait fabricators." These types of asymmetric media systems (Grossman and Hopkins 2016) may prompt forms of asymmetric affective polarization in ways that our measure misses. These asymmetries are unlikely to be unique to the United States: there is evidence from Western Europe that mainstream partisans dislike radical right parties more than radical right partisans reciprocally dislike mainstream parties (Helibling and Jungkunz 2020). Further examining affective asymmetries should feature on the agenda of comparative polarization scholars.

Our research joins an emerging literature that situates recent American political developments, especially the effects of intensifying polarization and populism, within a comparative perspective (e.g., Hawkins and Littvay 2019; Norris and Inglehart 2019; Levitsky and Ziblatt 2018; McCoy and Somer 2019; Westwood et al. 2018). Kuo (2019, 790) has recently noted that "political scientists are not trained to understand America in comparative perspective." We agree, but we also sense that this situation is changing. Initiating a dialogue between Americanist and comparative scholars of polarization requires rethinking theoretical concepts, collecting new data, and developing new measures of old concepts. We hope our work demonstrates the value of such efforts.

# References

Abou-Chadi, Tarik, and Markus Wagner. (2019). "The electoral appeal of party strategies in postindustrial societies: when can the mainstream left succeed?" *The Journal of Politics*, 81(4): 1405–1419.

Abramowitz, Alan, and Steven Webster. (2016). "The rise of negative partisanship and the nationalization of U.S. elections in the 21st century." *Electoral Studies*, *41*(C): 12–22.

Abramowitz, Alan, and Steven Webster. (2017). "The ideological foundations of affective polarization in the US electorate." *American Politics Research*, 45(4):621–647.

Adams, James. (2012). "Causes and electoral consequences of party policy shifts in multiparty elections: theoretical results and empirical evidence." *Annual Review of Political Science*, 15: 401–419.

Adams, James, Luca Bernardi, Lawrence Ezrow, Oakley B. Gordon, Tzu-Ping Liu, and M. Christine Phillips. (2019). "A problem with empirical studies of party policy shifts: alternative measures of party shifts are uncorrelated." *European Journal of Political Research*, 58(4): 1234–1244.

Altiparmakis, Argyrios. (2019). Greece – Punctuated Equilibrium: The Restructuring of Greek Politics. In Swen Hutter and Hanspeter Kriesi (eds.), *European Party Politics in Times of Crisis*. New York: Cambridge University Press, 95–117.

Anderson, Christopher J., and Christine A. Guillory. (1997). "Political institutions and satisfaction with democracy: A cross-national analysis of consensus and majoritarian systems." *American Political Science Review*, 91(1): 66–81.

Anton, Michael. (2016). "The Flight 93 election." *Claremont Review of Books*, Digital Edition, September 5, 2016.

Bakker, Ryan, Catherine de Vries, Erica Edwards et al. (2015). "Measuring party positions in Europe: The Chapel Hill expert survey trend file, 1999–2010." *Party Politics*, 21(1): 143–152.

Baldassarri, Delia, and Andrew Gelman. (2008). "Partisans without constraint: political polarization and trends in american public opinion." *American Journal of Sociology*, *114*(2), 408–446.

Bale, Tim, Paul Webb, and Monica Poletti. (2019). Party Members. In Anand Menon (ed.). *Brexit and Public Opinion*. The UK in a Changing Europe, 27–28.

Bankert, Alexa. (2020). "Negative and positive partisanship in the 2016 US presidential elections." *Political Behavior*.

Benkler, Yochai, Robert Faris, and Hal Roberts. (2018). *Network Propaganda: Manipulation, Disinformation, and Radicalization in American Politics.* Oxford: Oxford University Press.

Bonica, Adam. (2014). "Mapping the ideological marketplace." *American Journal of Political Science*, 58(2): 367–386.

Bonikowski, Bart. (2017). "Ethno-nationalist populism and the mobilization of collective resentment." *The British Journal of Sociology*, 68: S181–S213.

Bonikowski, Bart, Yuval Feinstein, and Sean Bock. (2019). *The Polarization of Nationalist Cleavages and the 2016 US Presidential Election.* Annual meeting of the American Political Science Association, Washington, DC.

Bormann, Nils-Christian, and Matt Golder. (2013). "Democratic electoral systems around the world, 1946–2011." *Electoral Studies*, 32(2): 360–369

Boxell, Levi, Matthew Gentzkow, and Jesse M. Shapiro. (2020). Cross-Country Trends in Affective Polarization. No. w26669. National Bureau of Economic Research.

Bremer, Björn, Swen Hutter, and Hanspeter Kriesi. (2020). "Dynamics of protest and electoral politics in the Great Recession." *European Journal of Political Research.*

Carlin, Ryan E., and Gregory J. Love. (2018). "Political competition, partisanship and interpersonal trust in electoral democracies." *British Journal of Political Science*, 48(01): 115–139.

Carmines, Edward G., and Nicholas J. D'Amico. (2015). "The new look in political ideology research." *Annual Review of Political Science*, *18*(1): 205–216.

Clark, Michael. (2009). "Valence and electoral outcomes in Western Europe, 1976–1998." *Electoral Studies*, 28(1): 111–122.

Clarke, Harold, Dutt Nitish, and Allan Kornberg. (1993). "The political economy of attitudes toward polity and society in west European democracies." *Journal of Politics*, 55(4): 998–1021.

Converse, Philip E., and Gregory B. Markus. (1979). "Plus c̦ a change: The new CPS Election Study Panel." *The American Political Science Review*, 73(1): 32–49.

Cramer, Katherine J. (2016). *The Politics of Resentment: Rural Consciousness in Wisconsin and the Rise of Scott Walker.* Chicago: University of Chicago Press.

da Silva, Frederico Ferreira, and Mariana S. Mendes. (2019). Portugal: A Tale of Apparent Stability and Surreptitious Transformation. In Swen Hutter and Hanspeter Kriesi (eds.), *European Party Politics in Times of Crisis*. Cambridge: Cambridge University Press, 139–164.

de Vries, Catherine, Armen Hakhverdian, and Bram Lancee. (2013). "The dynamics of voters' left/right identification: The role of economic and cultural attitudes." *Political Science Research and Methods*, 1(02): 223–238.

Druckman, James N., Samara Klar, Yanna Krupnikov, Matthew Levendusky, and John B. Ryan. (2020). "How Affective Polarization Shapes Americans' Political Beliefs: A Study of Response to the COVID-19 Pandemic." Journal of Experimental Political Science.

Druckman, James, and Matthew Levendusky. (2019). "What do we measure when we measure affective polarization?" *Public Opinion Quarterly*, 83(1): 114–122.

Druckman, James, S .R. Gubitz, Matthew S. Levendusky, and Ashley M. Lloyd. (2019). "How incivility on partisan media (de)polarizes the electorate." *Journal of Politics*, 81(1): 291–295.

Druckman, James, Samara Klar, Yanna Krupnikov, Matthew Levendusky and John Barry Ryan. *How Affective Polarization Shapes Americans' Political Beliefs: A Study of Response to the COVID-19 Pandemic*. Working paper.

Drutman, Lee. (2019). *Breaking the Two-Party Doom Loop: The Case for Multiparty Democracy in America*. Oxford: Oxford University Press.

Ellis, Christopher, and James A. Stimson. (2012). *Ideology in America*. Cambridge: Cambridge University Press.

Fiorina, Morris, Samuel Abrams, and Jeremy Pope. (2005). *Culture War? The Myth of a Polarized America*. New York: Pearson-Longman.

Fortunato, David, and Randolph T. Stevenson. (2013). "Perceptions of Partisan Ideologies: The Effect of Coalition Participation." American Journal of Political Science 57(2): 459–477.

Funke, Manuel, Moritz Schularick, and Christoph Trebesch. (2016). "Going to extremes: Politics after financial crises, 1870–2014." *European Economic Review*, 88: 227–260.

Gerring, John. (2012). "Mere description." *British Journal of Political Science*, 42(4): 721–746.

Gidron, Noam, James Adams, and Will Horne. (2019a). "Toward a comparative research agenda on affective polarization in mass publics." *APSA Comparative Politics Newsletter* 29: 30–36.

Gidron, Noam, James Adams, and Will Horne. (2019b) Who Dislikes Whom? The Drivers of Mass-Level Affective Polarization in Western Democracies. Annual Meeting of the American Political Science Association, Washington, DC.

Gidron, Noam, and Peter A. Hall. (2017). "The politics of social status: Economic and cultural roots of the populist right.'" *The British Journal of Sociology* 68: S57--S84.

Gidron, Noam, and Peter A. Hall. (2020). "Populism as a problem of social integration." *Comparative Political Studies*, 53(7):1027–1059.

Gilens, Martin. (1999). *Why Americans Hate Welfare: Race, Media, and the Politics of Antipoverty Policy.* Chicago: Chicago University Press.

Gilley, Bruce. (2006). "The meaning and measure of democratic legitimacy." *European Journal of Political Research*, 45(3): 499–525.

Goren, Paul, and Christopher Chapp. (2017). "Moral power: How public opinion on culture war issues shapes partisan predispositions and religious orientations." *American Political Science Review*, 111(1): 110–128.

Grossmann, Matt, and David A. Hopkins. (2016). *Asymmetric Politics: Ideological Republicans and Group Interest Democrats.* Oxford: Oxford University Press.

Hager, Sandy Brian. (2018). "Varieties of Top Incomes?" *Socio-Economic Review.*

Hall, Peter. (2020). "The electoral politics of growth regimes." *Perspectives on Politics* 18(1): 185–199.

Hare, Christopher, Keith T. Poole, and Howard Rosenthal. (2014). Polarization in Congress Has Risen Sharply: Where Is It Going Next? Wash. Post Monkey Cage Blog, Feb. 13. www.washingtonpost.com/news/monkey-cage/wp/2014/02/13/polarization-in-congress-has-risen-sharply-where-is-it-going-next/

Harteveld, Eelco. (2019). *Affective Polarization and Social Sorting Beyond the US: A Comparative Study.* Paper presented at the APSA annual meeting, Washington, DC.

Hawkins, Kirk, and Levente Littvay. (2019). Contemporary US Populism in Comparative Perspective. Cambridge: Cambridge University Press.

Helbling, Marc, and Sebastian Jungkunz. (2020). "Social divides in the age of globalization." *West European Politics* 43(6): 1187–1210.

Hetherington, Marc J. (2009). "Review article: Putting polarization in perspective." *British Journal of Political Science*, 39(02): 413–436.

Hetherington, Marc J., and Thomas J. Rudolph. (2015) *Why Washington Won't Work: Polarization, Political Trust, and the Governing Crisis.* Chicago: University of Chicago Press.

Hetherington, Marc J., Meri T. Long, and Thomas J. Rudolph. (2016). "Revisiting the myth: New evidence of a polarized electorate." *Public Opinion Quarterly*, 80: 321–350.

Hetherington, Marc, and Jonathan Weiler. (2018). *Prius Or Pickup? How the Answers to Four Simple Questions Explain America's Great Divide.* New York: Houghton Mifflin.

Hillygus, D. Sunshine, and Todd G. Shields. (2008). *The Persuadable Voter: Wedge Issues in Presidential Campaigns.* Princeton: Princeton University Press.

Hitlin, Steven, and Sarah K. Harkness. (2017). *Unequal Foundations: Inequality, Morality, and Emotions Across Cultures.* Oxford: Oxford University Press.

Hobolt, Sara B., and James Tilley. (2016). "Fleeing the centre: The rise of challenger parties in the aftermath of the euro crisis." *West European Politics* 39(5): 971–991.

Hobolt, Sara, Thomas J. Leeper, and James Tilley. (2020). "Divided by the vote: Affective polarization in the wake of the Brexit referendum.'" *British Journal of Political Science.*

Hooghe, Liesbet and Gary Marks. (2018). "Cleavage theory meets Europe's crises: Lipset, Rokkan, and the transnational cleavage." *Journal of European Public Policy*, 25(1): 109–135.

Huddy, Leonie, Lilliana Mason and Lene Aaroe. (2015). "Expressive partisanship: Campaign involvement, political emotion, and partisan identity." *American Political Science Review*, 109(1): 1–17.

Huddy, Leonie, Alexa Bankert, and Caitlin Davies. (2018). "Expressive versus instrumental partisanship in multiparty european systems." *Political Psychology*, *39*(3): 173–199.

Hutter, Swen, Argyrios Altiparmakis, and Guillem Vidal. (2019). Diverging Europe: The Political Consequences of the Crises in a Comparative Perspective. In Swen Hutter and Hanspeter Kriesi (eds.), *European Party Politics in Times of Crisis.* New York: Cambridge University Press, 329–354.

Iversen, Torben, and Soskice, David. (2015). "Information, inequality, and mass polarization: Ideology in advanced democracies." *Comparative Political Studies*, 48(13): 1781–1813.

Iyengar, Shanto, Gaurav Sood, and Yphtach Lelkes. (2012). "Affect, not ideology." *Public Opinion Quarterly*, 76(3): 405–431.

Iyengar, Shanto, and Sean Westwood. (2014). "Fear and loathing across party lines: New evidence on group polarization." *American Journal of Political Science*, 59(3): 690–707.

Iyengar, Shanto, Yphtach Lelkes, Matthew Levendusky, Neil Malhorta, and Sean Westwood. (2019). "The origins and consequences of affective polarization in the United States." *Annual Review of Political Science*, 22: 129–146.

Kalmoe, Nathan, and Lilliana Mason. (2019). *Lethal Mass Partisanship: Prevalence, Correlates, & Electoral Contingencies.* Washington, DC: NCAPSA American Politics Meeting.

Kinder, Donald R., and Nathan P. Kalmoe. (2017). *Neither Liberal nor Conservative: Ideological Innocence in the American Public.* Chicago: University of Chicago Press.

Kitschelt, Herbert. (1994). *The Transformation of European Social Democracy*. New York: Cambridge University Press.

Klar, Samara, Yanna Krupnikov, and John B. Ryan. (2018). "Affective polarization or partisan disdain?" *Public Opinion Quarterly*, 82(2): 379–390.

Klein, Ezra. (2020). *Why We're Polarized*. New York: Simon and Schuster.

Kriesi, Hans-Peter, Edgar Grande, Romain Lachat, Martin Dolezal, Simon Bornschier, and Timotheos Frey. (2008). *West European Politics in the Age of Globalization*. New York: Cambridge University Press.

Kriesi, Hanspeter. (2015). "Conclusion: The political consequences of the polarization of Swiss politics." *Swiss Political Science Review* 21(4): 724–739.

Kriesi, Hanspeter, and Swen Hutter. (2019). Crises and the Transformation of the National Political Space in Europe. In Swen Hutter and Hanspeter Kriesi (eds.), *European Party Politics in Times of Crisis*. New York: Cambridge University Press, 3–32.

Kuo, Didi. (2014). Electoral System Reform in the United States. Presented at the Program on American Democracy in Comparative Perspective, Stanford.

Kuo, Didi. (2019). "Comparing America: Reflections on democracy across subfields." *Perspectives on Politics*, 17(3): 788–800.

Lauka, Alban, Jennifer McCoy, and Rengin B. Firat. (2018). "Mass partisan polarization: Measuring a relational concept." *American Behavioral Scientist* 62(1): 107–126.

Lelkes, Yphtach. (2016). "Mass polarization: Manifestations and measurements." *Public Opinion Quarterly*, 80(S1): 392–410.

Lelkes, Yphtach. (2019). Policy over Party: Comparing the Effects of Candidate Ideology and Party on Affective Polarization. *Political Science Research and Methods*.

Lelkes, Yphtach, Gaurav Sood, and Shanto Iyengar. (2017) "The hostile audience: The effect of access to broadband internet on partisan affect." *American Journal of Political Science*, 61(1): 5–20.

Lelkes, Yphtach and Sean Westwood. (2017). "The limits of partisan prejudice." *Journal of Politics*, 79(2),485–501.

Levendusky, Matthew. (2009). *The Partisan Sort: How Liberals Became Democrats And Conservatives Became Republicans*. Chicago: University of Chicago Press.

Levendusky, Matthew. (2010). "Clearer cues, more consistent voters: A Benefit of elite polarization." *Political Behavior* 32(1): 111–131.

Levendusky, Matthew. (2018). "Americans, not partisans: Can priming American national identity reduce affective polarization?" *The Journal of Politics* 80(1): 59–70.

Levitsky, Steven, and Daniel Ziblatt. (2018). *How Democracies Die*. New York: Crown.

Lieberman, Robert C., Suzanne Mettler, Thomas B. Pepinsky, Kenneth M. Roberts, and Richard Valelly. (2019). "The Trump Presidency and American Democracy: A Historical and Comparative Analysis." *Perspectives on Politics*, 17(2): 470–479.

Lijphart, Arend. (2010). *Patterns of Democracy: Government Forms and Performance in Thirty-Six Countries*, 2nd ed. New Haven: Yale University Press.

López, Edward J., and Carlos D. Ramírez. (2004). "Party polarization and the business cycle in the United States." *Public Choice*, 121(3): 413–430.

Lupton, Robert N., William M. Myers, and Judd R. Thornton. (2015). "Political sophistication and the dimensionality of elite and mass attitudes, 1980–2004." *The Journal of Politics*, 77(2): 368–380.

Lupu, Noam. (2015). "Party polarization and mass partisanship: A comparative perspective." *Political Behavior*, 37(2): 331–356.

Mason, Lilliana. (2015). "'I disrespectfully agree': The differential effects of partisan sorting on social and issue polarization." *American Journal of Political Science*, 59(1): 128–145.

Mason, Lilliana. (2018). *Uncivil Agreement: How Politics Became Our Identity*. Chicago: University of Chicago Press.

McCarty, Nolan, Keith T. Poole, and Howard Rosenthal. (2006). *Polarized America: The Dance of Ideology and Unequal Riches*. Cambridge: MIT Press.

McCarty, Nolan. (2019). *Polarization: What Everyone Needs to Know*. Oxford: Oxford University Press.

McConnell, Christopher, Yotam Margalit, Neil Malhotra, and Matthew Levendusky. (2018). "The economic consequences of partisanship in a polarized era." *American Journal of Political Science*, 62(1): 5–18.

McCoy, Jennifer, and Murat Somer. (2019). "Toward a theory of pernicious polarization and how it harms democracies: Comparative evidence and possible remedies." *The Annals of the American Academy of Political and Social Science*, 681(1): 234–271.

Mickey, Robert, Steven Levitsky, and Lucas Way. (2017). Is America still a democracy? *Foreign Affairs*, 20, 20–29.

Miller, Patrick R. and Pamela Johnston Conover. (2015). "Red and blue states of mind." *Political Research Quarterly*, 68(2): 225–239.

Mudde, Cas, and Cristóbal Rovira Kaltwasser. (2018). "Studying populism in comparative perspective." *Comparative Political Studies* 51(13): 1667–1693.

Norris, Pippa. (2005). *Radical Right*. New York: Cambridge University Press.

Norris, Pippa, and Ronald Inglehart. (2019). *Cultural Backlash: Trump, Brexit, And Authoritarian Populism*. New York: Cambridge University Press.

Orr, Lilla V., and Gregory A. Huber. (2020). "The policy basis of measured partisan animosity in the United States." *American Journal of Political Science* 64(3): 569–586.

Pierson, Paul, and Eric Schickler. (2020). Madison's constitution under stress: A developmental analysis of political polarization. *Annual Review of Political Science, 23*(1).

Pop-Eleches, Grigore, and Joshua A. Tucker. (2011). "Communism's shadow: Postcommunist legacies, values, and behavior." *Comparative Politics*, 43(4),379–408.

Reiljan, Andres. (2020). "Fear and loathing across party lines (also) in Europe: Affective polarisation in European party systems." *European Journal of Political Research* 59(2): 376–396.

Rogowski, Jon C., and Joseph L. Sutherland. (2015). "How ideology fuels affective polarization." *Political Behavior*, 38(2): 485–508.

Saez, Emmanuel. 2012. *Striking It Richer: The Evolution of Top Incomes in the United States*. Working paper.

Sheffer, Lior. (2020). "Partisan In-Group Bias Before and After Elections." *Electoral Studies*.

Schickler, Eric. (2016). *Racial Realignment: The Transformation of American Liberalism, 1932–1965*. Princeton: Princeton University Press.

Sides, John, Michael Tesler, and Lynn Vavreck. (2018). *Identity Crisis: The 2016 Presidential Campaign and the Battle for the Meaning of America*. Princeton: Princeton University Press.

Skocpol, Theda, and Vanessa Williamson. (2011). *The Tea Party and the Remaking of Republican Conservatism*. Oxford: Oxford University Press.

Solt, Frederick. (2016). "The Standardized World Income Inequality Database." http://fsolt.org/swiid/,

Stewart, Alexander J, Nolan McCarty, and Joanna J. Bryson. (2020). *Polarization under Rising Inequality and Economic Decline*. Working paper. https://arxiv.org/abs/1807.11477

Stokes, Donald E. (1963). "Spatial models of party competition." *American Political Science Review*, 57(2): 368–377.

Sunstein, Cass R. (2015). "Partyism." U. Chi. Legal F. (2015): 1–27.

Taagepera, Rein, and Matthew S. Shugart. (1989). "Designing electoral systems." *Electoral Studies*, 8(1): 49–58.

Tavits, Margit. (2007). "Principle vs. pragmatism: Policy shifts and political competition." *American Journal of Political Science*, 51(1): 151–165.

Tesler, Michael. (2016). *Post-Racial or Most-Racial? Race and Politics in the Obama Era*. Chicago: University of Chicago Press.

Tsfati, Yariv, and Lilach Nir. (2017). "Frames and reasoning: Two pathways from selective exposure to affective polarization." *International Journal of Communication*, 11: 22.

Volkens, Andrea. (2017). *The Manifesto Data Collection. Manifesto Project (MRG/CMP/MARPOR)*. Version 2017b. Berlin: Wissenschaftszentrum Berlin für Sozialforschung (WZB).

Voorheis, John, Nolan McCarty, and Boris Shor. (2015).*Unequal Incomes, Ideology and Gridlock: How Rising Inequality Increases Political Polarization*" Working paper.

Wagner, Markus. 2020. "Affective Polarization in Multiparty Systems." *Electoral Studies*.

Ward, Dalston G., and Margit Tavits. (2019). "How Partisan Affect Shapes Citizens' Perception of the Political World." *Electoral Studies*.

Westwood, Sean J., Shanto Iyengar, Stefaan Walgrave, Rafael Leonisio, Luis Miller, and Oliver Strijbis. (2018). "The tie that divides: Cross-national evidence of the primacy of partyism." *European Journal of Political Research*, 70(2): 542–522.

Weyland, Kurt, and Raúl L. Madrid (eds.). (2019). When Democracy Trumps Populism: European and Latin American Lessons for the United States. Cambridge: Cambridge University Press.

Zakharova, Maria, and Paul V. Warwick. (2014). "The sources of valence judgments: The role of policy distance and the structure of the left–right spectrum." *Comparative Political Studies*, 47(14): 2000–2025.

# Acknowledgments

For research assistance, we thank Sara Sadat Kazemian, Guy Mor, Yuval Sade and Roi Zur. For comments and feedback, we thank Tarik Abou-Chadi, David Bracken, Sam Fuller, Peter Hall, Eelco Harteveld, Jennifer Hochschild, Sara Sadat Kazemian, Kathleen Thelen, Zeynep Somer-Topcu, Omer Yair and the anonymous reviewers. Special thanks to our editor, Frances Lee, for her encouragement, support and advice throughout this project. This research was supported by the ISRAEL SCIENCE FOUNDATION (grant No. 1806/19).

Cambridge Elements ☰

# American Politics

## Frances E. Lee
*Princeton University*

Frances E. Lee is Professor of Politics at the Woodrow Wilson School of Princeton University. She is author of *Insecure Majorities: Congress and the Perpetual Campaign* (2016), *Beyond Ideology: Politics, Principles and Partisanship in the U.S. Senate* (2009), and coauthor of *Sizing Up the Senate: The Unequal Consequences of Equal Representation* (1999).

## About the Series

The Cambridge Elements Series in *American Politics* publishes authoritative contributions on American politics. Emphasizing works that address big, topical questions within the American political landscape, the series is open to all branches of the subfield and actively welcomes works that bridge subject domains. It publishes both original new research on topics likely to be of interest to a broad audience and state-of-the-art synthesis and reconsideration pieces that address salient questions and incorporate new data and cases to inform arguments.

# Cambridge Elements ☰

# American Politics

## Elements in the Series

A full series listing is available at: www.cambridge.org/core/series/elements-in-american-politics

Printed in the United States
By Bookmasters